THE COWBOYS' SECRET

A STORY ABOUT HAZING
Gabe Higgins, 1975–1995

By Ruth Harten

Order this book online at www.trafford.com/06-0324
or email orders@trafford.com

Most Trafford titles are also available at major online book retailers.

© Copyright 2008 Ruth Harten.
All rights reserved. No part of this publication may be reproduced, stored in a retrieval system, or transmitted, in any form or by any means, electronic, mechanical, photocopying, recording, or otherwise, without the written prior permission of the author.

Note for Librarians: A cataloguing record for this book is available from Library and Archives Canada at www.collectionscanada.ca/amicus/index-e.html

Printed in Victoria, BC, Canada.

ISBN: 978-1-4120-8568-7

We at Trafford believe that it is the responsibility of us all, as both individuals and corporations, to make choices that are environmentally and socially sound. You, in turn, are supporting this responsible conduct each time you purchase a Trafford book, or make use of our publishing services. To find out how you are helping, please visit www.trafford.com/responsiblepublishing.html

Our mission is to efficiently provide the world's finest, most comprehensive book publishing service, enabling every author to experience success. To find out how to publish your book, your way, and have it available worldwide, visit us online at www.trafford.com/10510

 www.trafford.com

North America & international
toll-free: 1 888 232 4444 (USA & Canada)
phone: 250 383 6864 ♦ fax: 250 383 6804 ♦ email: info@trafford.com

The United Kingdom & Europe
phone: +44 (0)1865 722 113 ♦ local rate: 0845 230 9601
facsimile: +44 (0)1865 722 868 ♦ email: info.uk@trafford.com

10 9 8 7 6 5 4

Then the Lord said to Cain,

"Where is Abel your brother?"

He [Cain] said, "I do not know.
   Am I my brother's keeper?"

And God said, "What have you done?

The voice of your brother's blood

Cries out to Me from the ground."

                    Genesis 4:9

ACKNOWLEDGEMENTS

I want to thank all my friends who have been so encouraging and prayed for me, including Carol Carney and the whole Healing Rooms team. Thanks to my Mom who was my editor, encourager, and had the greatest patience when I kept telling her I was done only to find I wasn't. Thanks to Kathy Stevens, Dante Cantrill and Darin Lindley, who all gave me editing suggestions. And, of course, my biggest thanks to a big God whose hand has been on me through all of this.

I dedicate this book to my son, Brian, to all the Kappa Sig brothers Gabe so dearly loved and regarded, and all of his close friends who so deeply loved him.

CONTENTS

INTRODUCTION 1

SECTION I: Gabe's Story
1. Pennies From Heaven 5
2. Last Glimpses 19
3. You're Pledging What? 21
4. The Tapping In 24
5. Planning The Concert And The Picnic 34
6. The Initiation They Called "Picnic" 41
7. To The River 61
8. The Search Begins 67
9. Final Thoughts 74
10. The Banshee Cry Of The Death Angel 76
11. I'm O.K. Mom, I'm O.K. 80
12. The Wake 88
13. Wish You Were Here 110
14. What Really Happened To Cowboys 115
15. Who's Son Will Be Next? 130
16. Kicked Off Campus 134
17. Lord Of The Flies 146
18. The Texas Cowboys' Reformation 159
19. The Helmet And The Pennies 162

SECTION II: HAZING
20. Hazing Defined 166
21. Bullying 174
22. Binge Drinking 176
23. Stories: Hazing Isn't "Just Good Clean Fun" .. 179
24. Problems At University Of Texas 189
25. Can Hazing Be Stopped? 200
26. Advice To Parents 204

EPILOGUE
Blowing In the Wind 207
Murky Waters 209
Footnotes 212

INTRODUCTION

I received a phone call out of the blue that Saturday afternoon at 5:30.
"Hello?"
"Hello, Mrs. Higgins. This is Brian Thorp, one of Gabe's friends at UT. Do you remember me?"
"Of course I remember you, Brian."
He continued: "Mrs. Higgins, we think Gabe drowned in a river last night. (Pause) He was with the Texas Cowboys group. I'm so sorry."
(Pause) "It's O.K., Brian." I'm thinking: This has got to be a prank. This is not happening. This is not true. It must be a fraternity joke of some kind.
"We're not sure what happened. All we know is that they looked for a long time and couldn't find him. No one knew how to get hold of you. We could only find Gabe's dad's telephone number. We've been calling him and he must not be home. So I came up to Gabe's room and found your number."
He paused. My mind whirred. *If this was true, why aren't the police calling me? Or a University of Texas official?* Nothing he said was registering. My mind was saying that this was not true, and yet, reality said it must be. But it couldn't be.
"Gabe was on a campout on the river near Bastrop. I'm so sorry this happened."
And again I said, "It's O.K., Brian." *I kept consoling him!*
"I'm really sorry. I know Gabe meant a lot to you."
I'm thinking: *What is he talking about? This can't be real. This is not happening.* Again I responded, "It's O.K., Brian. It's all right."
"Are you O.K.?"
"I'm all right."
(Pause) "O.K. I'll talk to you later."
"All right."

"Goodbye."

"Goodbye."

I hung the phone up and stood there for a moment in shock. Then I began to shake and fell on the floor in a ball holding my stomach, crying and groaning, yelling: "Oh God, No. No, No, please, not Gabie! No, No, please not Gabie!" over and over.

My son, Gabriel (Gabe) Higgins was nineteen years old, a sophomore at the University of Texas in Austin. He drowned fully clothed wearing cowboy boots in the Colorado River 30 miles southeast of Austin, in the early morning of April 29, 1995, during an initiation into the Texas Cowboys organization. His blood alcohol level was 0.21.

This is Gabe's story.

It is not my desire to punish the Texas Cowboy Organization or the boys who were present that fateful night. I have changed the names of some of the officers in the Texas Cowboys organization and a couple of the names of his friends in an effort to protect them.

The simple definition of hazing is that it is the wrongful act of initiation. Any initiation that requires a person to perform a task that is demeaning, dangerous, silly or ridiculous and is part of the process for admission into *any* group can be labeled hazing.

It is my belief that if those who are in a position to make a difference do not take a stand, then we will by our inaction be condoning the crime.

It is my hope that this book will make a difference.

SECTION I

Gabe's Story

Gabe. Three years old

~1~

PENNIES FROM HEAVEN

The trip to Reno was a ten-hour drive and just like the year before at Christmastime, we played Twenty Questions across the Nevada desert. Gabe and I had both gotten pretty good at it from all the trips to Idaho Falls for Gabe's rehabilitation on his knee during his senior year of high school. We creatively changed the rules so that if it got too hard or began slowing down, we had to give a clue.

Gabe: "OK. It's mineral."
Me: "Is it bigger than a bread box?"
Gabe: "U-h-h-h, Yeah. I think so."
I asked, "Is it something that's in the car?"
He looked at me funny for a second, then cocked his head and replied, "Well, I don't know. Probably not right now."
"Could it be at home?"
"Yeah, it could be."
"Is it in both places?" I asked.
"Yeah, It could be."
"Do I have one of these?"
"Yeah, on occasion."
"OK. Do you have one?"
"Y-e-e-a-a-h."
"Does Brian?" (Gabe's older brother)
"Oh yeah."
"Does your girlfriend, Crystal have one?"

"Uh-h-h-h. I guess maybe she does."
"So are there lots of these then? Do lots of people own these things?"
"Y-e-e-a-a-h."
"All right. So these are good things then?"
Hesitating a moment, he answered, "It depends on where you sit!"
He laughs.
Sit? Now I'm really confused. It's not supposed to be this hard. "When do we use these things?" I asked, knowing he wouldn't answer because the rules say you can only answer "yes" or "no."
He doesn't answer. He just laughs again with a twinkle in his eye and says, "That's around ten or eleven, but who's counting?"
Long pause. I'm thinking: A mineral.
"Uhm. What color is it?"
No answer because it's not a yes or no answer.
"O.K. Is it Silver colored?"
"No."
"Gold?"
"No."
"Green?"
"U-h-h-h. Maybe."
I thought. *This could take all day.*
Gabe says: "Ask something else."
"O.K. Mineral. Is this a hard metal?"
"Nope."
"So is it like a gaseous mineral or something?"
"Yup."
"So, it's not a solid?"
"Nope."
I hesitated and thought for a moment. We were too much alike. I asked: "Does it smell really bad?"
He answered, "Y-y-y-u-u-p!"
"H-m-m-m," I said. "It's gaseous, green and smelly!" I paused. "How about: It starts with an f and rhymes with art?"
"You got it."
We belly laughed. That was tricky.
I began the next one: "O.K. It's mineral."
Gabe asked: "Is it larger than a bread box?"
Me: "Ye-e-a-a-h."

Gabe: "Is it bigger than the car?"
"No."
Gabe: "Is it in the car?"
"No."
"Is it at home?"
"Yeah."
"Is it something I own?"
"No."
"Is it something you own?"
"Yeah."
"Is it silver?"
"Yeah."
"Is it your flute?"
"Yeah."

With the easy ones out of the way, we started on the hard ones, like the clouds, the yellow line down the middle of the road, and the Tasmanian devil. A couple hours flew by. It was remarkably good weather. The year before it had been snowing when we reached the middle of Nevada. Finally, I put the seat back and took a nap. Gabe kept driving and listened to his music with earphones so I could sleep.

As I woke up, I laid motionless, in love with the moment of time I was in. It was so great being with my son. It had been a year since I'd seen him last. Memories flooded over me. He had been such a delightful child. Even as a baby, he would sing himself to sleep at night and wake up playing and singing in the morning.

Gabe was born in San Diego, which we considered to be one of the best places the Navy had to offer. Tim, his dad, was a student pilot at Miramar Naval Air Station and I taught in the San Diego Swim Program. Gabe was six-months old when I began teaching him to swim in our hot tub.

We were in San Diego ten months before Tim was given orders to fly F4s off the Midway Aircraft Carrier out of Yokosuka, Japan. One week later he left. I sold the car, rented the house, packed up and a month later the kids and I were in Japan. We didn't see Tim for months until the ship pulled in at Christmastime. A month later we moved to Yokohama, the larger of the two Navy housing areas, which was an hour's drive north of Yokosuka where the ship was based.

The housing area was located on a bluff overlooking the city. Our quadrangle of grass was enclosed by three two-story four-plexes. In this grouping were three ten-year old boys and a mixture of children every age and size down to Gabie, who was two.

The kids would knock on our door and ask if Gabe could come out and play. They loved throwing the ball to him and playing with him; it didn't matter what kind of ball or what kind of game. His older brother, Brian was so involved in sports, it didn't take Gabe long to become somewhat savvy at baseball, soccer and football. We loved watching him waddle in his diapers, either kicking or running with a ball. He was amazingly coordinated and agile, even then. Brian's baseball games wouldn't be the same without little Gabie singing, "Hey batter! Batter – batter, whatsamatter."

When the Midway and her escorts were all in, it meant every family in the quad was a complete unit with a dad, a rare coincidence we all treasured. If, at that time, any of the dads wandered onto the quad in the late afternoon, he was fair game.

Like a swarm of bees coming out of their honeycomb, the kids would each magically appear from their houses and gather around, tumbling and tackling each other. The beehive now awakened would draw three or four more dads onto the quad, usually with a football. In a short time a full-fledged game would be in progress, including the cheering section of us moms.

I held Gabe back as long as I could, but to no avail. He eventually made it out onto the field with the rest of the beehive as if he knew as much and was equal in their strides. You'd think the game would have been too rough, but the guys had an extra sense, a Gentle Ben touch that included Gabe with hardly any effort. Yet it did take somewhat of a different flavor.

When Gabe got the ball it was a gratuitous gesture at best, because as most two year olds fare, he would take off with delight in a half-run, half-waddle for parts unknown, leaving all the dads and kids in awe that he could stop the whole football game. Then out of nowhere, his dad would run up from behind him, swoop him up in his arms, and run all the way to the goal line for a touchdown! A dad carrying a young child wasn't fair game for a tackle or even a swiped football. Everyone clapped and cheered. It was better therapy for all of us than any football game TV could have offered.

There were lots of pluses and minuses in the Navy. Not having a dad or any relatives around was probably the biggest negative. Birthdays without a dad were hard, and the frequent moves took their toll. Yet living in Japan and all over the United States were great adventures for all of us and we totally loved it.

After the tour in Japan, we moved to Orange Park, Florida where Tim became an A4 jet fighter pilot instructor. We had our dream house built and the kids and I went swimming every day all summer. That fall, we put both kids in school. Brian was in the fifth grade and Gabe was enrolled into Grace Lutheran preschool.

I was the first driver of the car pool of six kids. It went pretty smoothly that morning. However, the afternoon "pickup" didn't go as planned. I followed the protocol and walked up to the gate, asking the teacher for Car Pool Number Five.

She replied, "Just a moment, please," and walked back to the farthest bench where they were waiting. The children immediately stood up and followed her back to the gate like little ducklings following a mother duck. She opened the gate and they passed through as I counted them: "One, two, three, four, five. Wait! There's supposed to be six! One is missing!" I looked again at the children, "And it's mine!" I quickly hustled the kids into the car and rushed back.

By now, the entire place looked like a disturbed ant colony. All the teachers were in a panic. They looked in all four of the classrooms, under tables, in closets, outside on the playground, across the fence, everywhere. No Gabe. They called his name. Nothing. Time passed. All the carpoolers had come and gone and I was now standing there alone. I just watched everyone, thinking: *I just received a flyer that explained where the single car pickups were to pick their children up, which was the next building over in the gym. They labeled the little children who were to go there,* "Honeybees." *And Gabe's nickname at home is* "Honeybee." *I wonder ...*

I shared this with the teacher. Hope appeared on her harried face. She ran to the gym. Voila! Sweet little Gabie was happily playing with the single car pickup kids in the gym!

He came running out to me like nothing in the world was wrong and I assure you, I quickly realized that in his world, there was nothing wrong! He was just doing what they told him to do. The single car pickup lady had stuck her head in the classroom door and called: "All the little Honeybees come with me." And since Gabe was a little Honeybee, he followed her to the gym like a good little duckling.

I almost chuckled out loud. Then another sweet memory flew past me.

Our next tour of duty was in Key West, Florida where we lived in a small three bedroom Navy duplex on the water with our own boat dock. We all loved it. It was like being on vacation all the time. The kids had their own fort in the large rubber tree in the back yard. Tim tied a rope on the tree so the kids could swing over the water from the dock to the land. They spent hours fishing off the dock. We bought a sixteen-foot Hoby Cat Sailboat and a 23-foot motorboat and thought we were living in heaven.

The swimming pool was only a block away and the kids and I spent everyday all summer there, when we weren't out in one of the boats. Gabe swam like a fish. Both kids did. I taught them both how to swim and dive. I gave Gabe a quarter for every good dive. At the end of the summer, he was rich. He was the only four-year old they allowed in the deep end of the pool because he swam so well.

We had a lot of fun in Key West. Squadron parties, sunsets at Mallory Square, fishing trips, sailing the Hoby Cat, perpetual tans.

On the weekends we either went sailing or took the motorboat to Hemingway Stilts where there were prolific sand dollars, or to Lighthouse Key where there were tropical fish and nice little shells, or to Woman Key, an overnighter, when lobsters were in season. After our first year there, Gabe, at the age of five, became totally proficient like the rest of us at snorkeling, swimming, and diving down into the six to eight-feet-deep water around the stilts to scoop up sand dollars or sea biscuits.

Hemingway Stilts was a house on the water that Ernest Hemingway built in the 1940's about 4 to 5 miles northwest of Key West, an easy boat trip across somewhat shallow water. A hurricane had blown it down many years earlier, and all that was left were the huge iron supporting beams protruding from the water.

When we first started going there, there was a two-foot barracuda that had staked the area out as his own, which was fine with us as long as he kept his distance. The protocol was to pull up to the stilts and wait for him to circle the boat twice, after which he would disappear to the other side of the silts. My girlfriend nicknamed him, "Fred, the Friendly Barracuda."

Not so one day. After playing and swimming, we all climbed into the boat to have lunch. Gabe had fallen asleep on his smaller float raft, his flippers dangling over the edge into the water. The raft was attached to the boat by a 15-20 foot rope. When I sat down to eat my sandwich I saw Fred circling my little Gabie's float raft and screamed! We quickly reeled Gabe into the boat.

Toward the end of our two-year tour, Fred had grown over six feet, and the last time we were there, he was no more. Someone obviously no longer thought Fred was very friendly anymore.

Those were good years, but after Gabe finished the first grade, Tim and I talked about getting divorced. I moved back home to Pocatello, Idaho, bought a house and put the kids in school. (We eventually divorced).

Every fall it was a tradition in my family when the leaves began to turn, for all of us to pile into dad's station wagon and travel the 40-minute drive to Lava Hot Springs. We grew up spending many summer weekends swimming in the big pools, and winters soaking in the hot pools. The combination of being with family and soaking in the hot pools was always delightful and relaxing for all of us.

Afterwards, we went to our favorite restaurant for dinner. Gabe finished early and asked me for some change to buy some gum. I obliged, and as we left the restaurant, he took four pennies of change and threw them on the sidewalk.

I was appalled as I was on a limited budget and gasped in shock: "Gabe, what are you doing?"

He answered in a totally calm, logical demeanor, "Mom! Somebody's got to put the lucky pennies down!"

Years later I remarried and we moved to a little town in central Idaho named Mackay (rhymes with kaki). One day I walked out of the house and found four pennies on the sidewalk. I knew it was Gabe.

Gabe was in the seventh grade when we moved to Mackay. It was a delightful little town, one mountain range to the east of Sun Valley. I called it Idaho's best-kept secret. We loved it. Especially Gabe. He seemed to be more comfortable in a small school.

I was in an exercise class one night when Gabe came running into the building out of breath and asked me if I would pick up my things and come outside with him. I wasn't too happy about that and thought, "*Man, there better be a good reason for this, buddy.*"

We got outside and he told me that his stepbrother had just died (at the age of nineteen). Gabe, a sophomore in high school, was really affected by it. He flew off the next day for the funeral.

Gabe spent the summers with his dad back east. Between his sophomore and junior years, he was a counselor at a camp in Virginia for children with special needs.

One afternoon at the camp, he caught a young man bullying a younger boy. Gabe pulled the bully aside and verbally began to set him straight. All through lunch Gabe eyed the young man. One of the adult counselor's noticed what was happening and took Gabe for a walk. Gabe opened up to the counselor and told him that he didn't like abusive behavior and shared about his stepbrother who lost his long-term memory from a prescribed drug interaction. He'd died just the year before. The counselor consoled him. Gabe was fierce about protecting the less fortunate.

That summer, Gabe talked me into allowing him to live his junior year with his dad and step-mom in Galveston, Texas. I reluctantly did so. The summer after his junior year he worked for six weeks in Washington, D.C. as a page for Jack Brooks, Dem. Texas, in the U.S. House of Representatives (1992). He regarded that as an experience of a lifetime.

Gabe and his dad took one weekend that summer to drive over to Austin and look at the campus at University of Texas. Gabe fell in love with it and immediately decided that was where he wanted to go to school, even though his dad and step-mom were encouraging him to go to a private school back east.

A couple weeks before Gabe was to spend his senior year in Galveston, he broke his collarbone. After that healed, during the first practice back on the football field, he was running with the football, turned and popped his ACL ligament in his knee. The next week he was living with us in Mackay. His knee was operated on the day before Thanksgiving. He missed his whole senior year of playing sports, which was hard for him because he was very athletic.

Gabe graduated Salutatorian from Mackay High School on May 24th, 1993.

Even though things seemed to turn against Gabe, he still kept a positive attitude. In his graduation speech, he spoke warmly of his teachers, his parents and his friends. I am in awe of the strength of character that he walked in. He was always an encouragement to his friends, to his brother, and to me. He quoted Polonius' farewell speech in Shakespeare's <u>Hamlet</u>: "This above all: to thine own self be true. And it must follow, as the night the day: thou canst not then be false to any man. Farewell: my blessing season this in thee."

As I lay in the car cruising across Nevada, I thought that Gabe and I had weathered through a lot during his nineteen years. He was a great son to me. I remembered his graduation speech as though he was speaking it directly to me. After he graduated from high school, he worked through the summer for my younger brother in Pocatello. Then my older brother and I drove him to Salt Lake City to see him off on the plane to go to school at the University of Texas. It was bittersweet seeing him go, but I was confident that he would be OK, living only a couple hours from his dad and step-mom.

After he was gone, I left Jim and moved to Pocatello to finish my music degree.

When Gabe arrived that Christmas, I had just finished my finals. We made a trip to the mall and as we walked out Gabe stopped, reached into his pocket, pulled out a handful of change, picked out the pennies and tossed them onto the sidewalk.

I was in shock. "Are you still doing that?"

He chuckled: "Yeah, Mom! Somebody's got to put those lucky pennies down!"

We laughed together like two people who knew a secret no one else on earth knew. Then, slowly, we walked to the car in silence. It was so good being with him again.

(Clockwise)
Gabe. Four years old in Key West
Boogey Boarding with girlfriend Paige
Hoby Cat with Brian and Max
On the boat with Max the dog
On float raft asleep at Hemingway Stilts

(Clockwise)
Ruth, Brian and Gabe
Ruth and Gabe
Gabe the cookie icer at Christmas
Gabe playing guitar at home

Basketball and Track in Mackay, Idaho
Sophomore year in High School

Football #85 in Mackay, Idaho
Sophomore year in High School

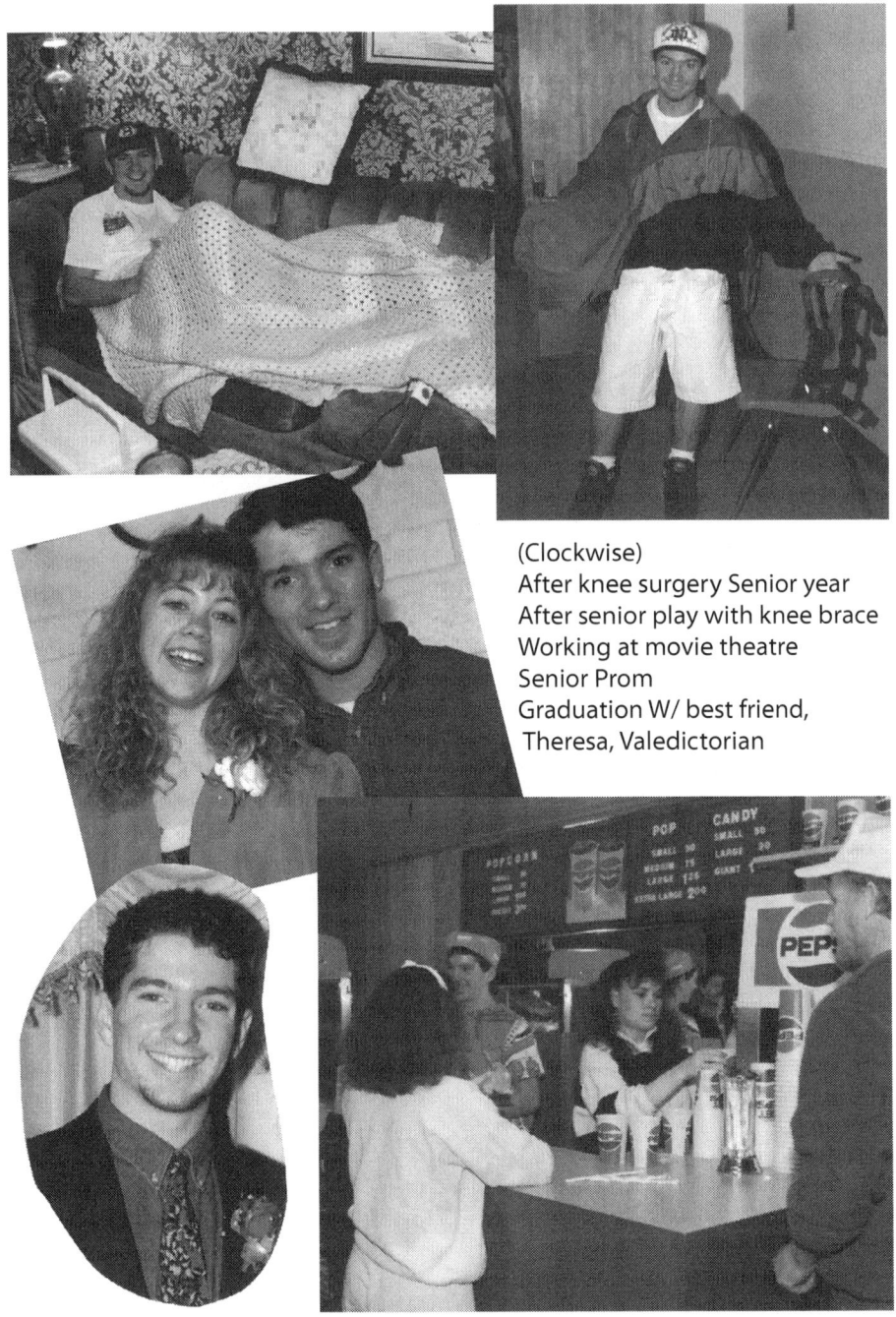

(Clockwise)
After knee surgery Senior year
After senior play with knee brace
Working at movie theatre
Senior Prom
Graduation W/ best friend,
 Theresa, Valedictorian

~2~

LAST GLIMPSES

This was the second Christmas that Gabe, Brian and I met at my sister Dorothy's house in Reno. It seemed to work really well meeting there.

At Dorothy's, Gabe told us all about school. "I really love going to school at the University of Texas. I don't ever wear a coat anymore. I wear shorts now. I think it's really funny, you can always tell who the freshmen are because they're the ones who are still wearing jeans!"

He continued: "I really love the Kappa Sigs. They're a great bunch of guys. I feel it's a real honor to belong to such a great fraternity. Several of the guys have been really cordial to me. I'm always getting invited over to dinner or for the weekend to watch a game or just hang out with their family."

It didn't take much urging to get him to show us pictures of his girlfriend, Crystal [not her real name]. "I just took her to the fraternity Christmas Party. She's really nice, Mom. You'd really like her. I just haven't decided if she's 'the one'."

Dorothy made a batch of cookies and we delegated Gabe to be the cookie icer. The rule was that if the cookie was broken, you could eat it. There were no rules that said you couldn't break one of the cookies.

Before Dorothy's husband got home from work, we were talking in the kitchen. Dorothy was cooking while I fed little two year-old Aimee. There was a rare moment of silence between us and we looked over into the family room where Gabe was watching a football game on TV, holding the baby. We hadn't heard six-month old Josh wake up. Gabe was saying to him, "So, Josh! Who do you think's gonna win the Super Bowl this year? I personally think the San Francisco 49ers have an excellent chance at it. They seem to have a really good team this year and I like their quarterback … " Josh was transfixed on every word and even though he was probably hungry, not a sound of discontent came from him. Dorothy and I smiled at each other and without saying a word, agreed that Gabe was a really neat young man.

Brian's car pulled up late that night, and the next day we exchanged gifts and caught up on all the news. For the first time in their lives, I saw a deeper bonding and love growing between these two brothers. They were never really at odds with each other, but until now, they lived in two different worlds since they were seven years apart. Now at last, their worlds were beginning to come together. The only subject they couldn't talk about with any ease was fraternities. Brian was adamantly against them. He saw no good in them and thought they were a waste of time and money. But he knew Gabe loved his fraternity, so out of respect they talked about other things like girls, football, computers, and motorcycles.

The vacation ended all too soon and after seeing Brian off, Gabe and I said our goodbyes to Dorothy and her family and drove back to Pocatello.

A week later, my older brother, Don and I drove Gabe to Salt Lake City and put him on a plane to Austin. The night before he left, we stayed at our cousin's house and played cards, ending with our favorite, Indian Poker. For some odd reason, I took pictures of everyone. They were the last pictures I took of Gabe.

The next day we said our goodbyes at the airport and though I was sad to see him leave, I had no idea that it would be the last time I would ever see him alive.

~3~

YOU'RE PLEDGING WHAT?

Gabe was busy with school that spring semester as was I. Over the Christmas vacation, we had discussed the whole issue of his father paying for his education. His dad had given him an ultimatum at the end of his freshman year: If his grades didn't pick up significantly, he wouldn't pay for any more of Gabe's college education. That summer between Gabe's freshman and sophomore years, he had produced a B and two C's, which wasn't acceptable to his dad.

Two days before the fall semester of Gabe's sophomore year, his dad told him that he wouldn't pay for any more of his schooling. He suggested Gabe move to Galveston and go to a Community College, or move to Idaho and go to college here. Gabe called me, very upset. It was his desire to stay in school at UT at any cost.

Single and going to school myself, I had no money to give or even lend him. My folks loaned him a thousand dollars and the Kappa Sig president extended himself and told him he could live at the fraternity house all semester if he paid his room and board at the end of the semester. He agreed to. Everything else was put on his charge card.

He elected to prove himself by bringing his grades up in hopes that his father would have a change of heart. It was a huge gamble, but he felt he had to do it.

After Christmas vacation Gabe found out he'd received 2 A's, 2 B's, and a C which was a good enough GPA to satisfy his dad, who paid all his debt, room and board, and his fraternity dues a semester ahead.

Gabe immediately called me and told me the good news.

Toward the end of January, he called again and told me about another fraternity he was thinking about joining, called "The Texas Cowboys." I thought to myself: *"How much more involving could a second fraternity be? It couldn't possibly be very active or time-consuming or they wouldn't allow it on campus."* He explained that it was a local fraternity composed of guys from other fraternities and a few non-fraternity independents.

I knew that the Kappa Sigs already took up a lot of Gabe's time. I figured this new fraternity might probably take about as much time as maybe, chess club or something. After all, they didn't even have a building. I mean, the main reason he was there was to go to school, right?

He said, "Mom, if I joined the Texas Cowboys, I could just about name my own job after I graduated. The Texas Cowboys is a well-known and influential fraternity and only the best belong to this group. It's an elite spirit and service fraternity, and they shoot the cannon off at the football games. One day, I might even be on TV."

I personally felt that it was a contradiction for Gabe to want to be a Texas Cowboy. Only a few years earlier in the small town of Mackay, tucked away in the beautiful Idaho mountains and surrounded by ranches, known for their weekly rodeos throughout the summer, you would *never* have caught Gabe dressing like a cowboy. We only went to one rodeo. He was just not into it.

It may have had something to do with the fact that a cowboy's life in Idaho is quite different from one in Texas. In Idaho cowboys spend the months of January and February birthing the newborn calves in sub-zero temperatures. Frequent blizzards make it a hard life, and it doesn't pay well, unless you own the ranch.

"Cool" was not "Cowboy" to the Gabe I knew.

In high school, Gabe seemed to have had a conflict going on between "East Coast sophisticated" and the laid back, Western-easy-going cowboy life style Mackay presented. Before going to college, it was pretty clear that Gabe had chosen the East Coast thing.

However, a month or two into school at the beginning of his freshman year at UT, he called me up excited and said: "Mom, you'll never guess what I did! I just bought a cowboy hat, cowboy boots, belt and buckle, and cowboy shirt, AND, I'm even listening to cowboy music now."

I was in shock and couldn't speak.

He laughed and added, "And Mom. The babes love it!!"

It was monumental in Gabe's life. He had chosen a lifestyle fitting both East Coast and Western. Something in the middle: A sophisticated cowboy who looked real good. O.K. Who looked real good "to the babes."

I accepted that Gabe had changed and maybe there was something charming about being a prestigious Texas Cowboy. His excitement was undeniably contagious. I honestly didn't think a whole lot about it at first. I just trusted his judgment. In a short time I became more concerned about his ability to concentrate on his studies in school and told him so.

~4~

THE TAPPING IN

TEXAS COWBOY SELECTION

To be a Texas Cowboy, a young man had to be a sophomore in good standing with 36 semester hours, a 2.5 grade point average, showing good character and leadership qualities.

Each prospective cowboy pledge submitted a written application, followed by an interview with the Dean of Students. A selection committee then read through the applications and made their selections. In the fall, there was generally one applicant from each participating fraternity and in the spring, there were two each. They also allowed a few applicants who were not in any fraternities, labeled independents.

As soon as the Dean of Students made the Cowboy pledge selections, the fraternities were notified. The Texas Cowboys in each fraternity would tell their newly chosen Cowboy pledges that they had been selected and to get ready to be "tapped in."

THE TAPPING IN

On the day of the *tap-in*, the Kappa Sig Cowboys told Gabe and his fraternity pledge partner, John Welsh, that they had been accepted as pledges and that they should go get drunk because the tapping in ceremony would involve a paddling and that it was going to hurt. Gabe did just that. He got drunk. According to his roommate, he drank a six-pack of Busch Lite and a bottle of bourbon. He "wanted to be pretty drunk," because he "didn't want to feel it." [1]

One might think that a *tap-in* would involve a tapping on the shoulder to tell the pledge that he had been accepted into the organization (as a pledge). Maybe that's what it originally meant, I don't know. For the Texas Cowboys it was another term for paddling.

The ones who administered the paddlings for Gabe's *tap-in* were his older Kappa Sigma brothers. Four Cowboys fell into that category. Later I found it odd that the very same Kappa Sigs that talked him into pledging and convinced him about how wonderful the Cowboys were, were the same ones who participated in paddling him for the *tap-in*. [2]

Gabe told his girlfriend that the first 5 or 6 "licks," or paddlings, hurt like hell. He wanted to cry. After that he was so numb that he couldn't feel it. He was paddled 19 or 20 times.

After the paddling, they had a party to honor the pledges. Pictures of Gabe were taken that night at the party. One particular picture shocked me because I'd never seen such a look of so much pain on his face. [Picture enclosed]

Later that night he called a close friend, a girl, sometime between 1:00 and 2:00 in the morning. She was asleep. Her roommate, who was up watching TV, answered the phone. Gabe asked if it was okay if he came over and if she could wake up his friend, Georgia. She said, "Sure."

When he got to her apartment, he kept telling her over and over, "You can't tell anyone. Please don't tell anyone."

He told her "They paddled us tonight and I'm in major pain." On the verge of tears, he kept saying, "You don't understand how much pain I'm in."

Gabe asked her to hold him. He was very drunk, but coherent. She said she knew he was coherent because he had asked her to wake him up at 8:00 a.m. and she had forgotten to. He'd overslept and asked her the next morning why she hadn't awakened him at 8:00.

There was no physical attachment between these two close friends since they were both involved with other people. She let him sleep in one of the twin beds while she slept in the other bed, her roommate on the couch. At his request, she laid next to him on top of the blanket until he fell asleep, his arm tucked under her head.

Gabe, like many Texas Cowboy Newmen pledges, did not sit down for one to two weeks. Many times in intense pain he stood at the back of his classes.

Gabe's girlfriend, Crystal, who lived in Dallas, was in Austin two weeks after the *tap-in*. He was still so sore that he had trouble getting up and down, from sitting to standing. She couldn't believe it and asked to see his rear end. He showed her. She told me later that there were big black spots all over his "buns," maybe ten of them.

When Gabe first became a Cowboy, he was very excited. He told Crystal he thought that, as a Cowboy, he would be doing something good for others and that it made him feel good. As time lapsed, he became more and more despondent with the Cowboys. He talked about getting out of it and was always miserable.

According to his roommate even the week before the initiation he was running around doing Cowboy stuff and coming in at 3:00 a.m. When I first heard this, I thought his roommate meant that he was out trying to raise money for the Cowboys. Later I realized that he wasn't out until three in the morning selling ads, he was out being hazed.

A short time after the *tap-in*, Gabe petitioned the Engineering Department to drop one of his classes in order to devote more time to pledging the Texas Cowboys. They approved it and he cut his hours down to a class load of ten credits.

THE ARC

As part of the pledging requirements, Gabe worked one hour a week at the ARC, the Austin Retarded Citizens, also called the Rosedale School. This was a school for handicapped and mentally challenged children, kindergarten through high school. When he told me about it and that he played the guitar for them, I imagined him playing in front of a fifth grade classroom of possibly ten to twelve children who were mildly mentally challenged. Not so.

Gabe sang and played his guitar each week for Robin Gurke's class of around seven young children between the ages of three and six who were severely handicapped. The children loved the music, as did the teacher and her assistant. The class would calm down and listen as he played and sang, "their expressions priceless." Gabe loved playing for them so much through the semester and had connected with them so well, that he brought his friends with him a few times to meet the kids.

Since it was an all day school, Robin Gurke and her aide would feed each child every day. Some of these feedings paralleled a mother feeding a six-month old baby. At least one child gurgled, breathing loudly as he struggled with each breath through the feedings. Mrs. Gurke and her assistant had to be prepared to handle every kind of situation, occasionally requiring a 911-phone call while performing CPR until the ambulance arrived.

Part of the reason that Gabe loved to volunteer at the ARC probably had something to do with his stepbrother's death, which left a passion in Gabe to help those who were less fortunate, especially those with mental impairments.

Mrs. Gurke told me later that she liked Gabe's music and appreciated his visits – also that he sounded lots better at the end of the semester than at the beginning.

RAISING MONEY

The Texas Cowboy pledge class that semester had 30 pledges: basically, a composite of two from each participating fraternity plus four independent students. The money the Texas Cowboys donated to the ARC each semester was $15,000, which was presented at the spring concert the end of April and at the fall concert.

The money was raised from the ads the pledges sold: a full-page ad ran $100, half page was $50, and a quarter page was $25. Then the ads were put into an 8 x 10 inch booklet and sold at the concert.

The Cowboys sponsored two concerts a year: the Harvest Moon in the fall and the Spring Music Festival. They have showcased such entertainers as The Temptations, Dwight Yoakum, Merle Haggard, Jerry Jeff Walker, Stevie Ray Vaughn, Waylon Jennings, Larry Gatlin, Dolly Parton, and Joe Diffie.

At the weekly Wednesday night pledge meeting, the Cowboy initiates, labeled Newmen, were told they were expected to raise a certain amount each week. Testimonies stated that the money was a "targeted amount" or an "optional, suggested amount," which was intentionally set too high for most of the pledges to make. The premise of setting the amount too high was so that when they failed to meet that quota, it gave good reason for the Cowboys to haze them the following weekend. Gabe often shared this information with his group of close friends because he was so stressed about it. [3]

When the Cowboys' president and pledge trainer were Newmen together, they were given "targeted amounts" of only $250-300 a week, while the majority of the others were told to raise amounts of $500 and higher. In the answers to interrogatories, one of the officers admitted that they had raised at total of $2200, or an average of $200 a week. [4]

Another active's statement said: "the Cowboy pledges were required to sell $800 of ads per week but usually everyone sold only $600." [5]

At the beginning of each Wednesday meeting the pledges would hand in the money from the previous week. Then the pledges waited outside the meeting room while the officers decided on the required amounts of money that each set of pledges were to raise for the following week. Each duo of fraternity pledges would be separately called in and told the amount they needed to raise for the next week.

Gabe told me in February that both he and his pledge mate John were told they were expected to raise $6,000 to $7,000 together over a ten-week period from the second week of February to the third week of April.

Two of Gabe's friends explained to me that it was their understanding that if any of the Newmen pledges didn't make their quotas for one week (i.e.: turning in $590 instead of $600), they would receive a black X beside their names. They were told that if any of them received three black X's, they were out of the Cowboys.

According to Gabe, he and John had received one "X." One time Gabe and John were the only Cowboy pledges who made their quota and everyone else got a black "X." One other week none of the thirty pledges made their quotas.

Gabe and John were expected to raise approximately $600 each week. The last two weeks the requirement became $800 each week. In order to raise $600 a week, one would have to sell six $100 ads, twelve $50 ads, twenty-four $25 ads, or any combination of the above.

Gabe confided to me on the phone that though he and John were friends, they didn't work very closely with each other. He told me in early April that he was disappointed with John, in fact angry with him for his lack of involvement raising the money, which left Gabe more burdened to earn more than his half of the quotas. According to John's statement, however, they split the money down the middle. Gabe told me on the phone that he thought a large portion of the money John gave to the Cowboys was from an inheritance he had received from his grandfather. Though a lot of the Cowboys worked hard for the money they earned, many of the wealthier Newmen only needed to ask their families for the money each week.

It became harder for Gabe to find a business around the university that hadn't already taken out an ad. He borrowed a friend's truck almost every afternoon in order to drive to businesses farther away from the university to solicit them for ads. The second reason he drove so far from the campus was probably because he was told that if any of the Cowboy actives saw him off campus, he would be hazed the following weekend.

Gabe was angry and very stressed out that he had to work so hard. Toward the end of the semester, he had over $1000 of his own money into it. He asked me several times through the semester for money. I sent him $100 each month for his phone bill, but none of it went toward the phone bill. It all went into the Texas Cowboy's fund. None of the money I sent him produced any ads, either. He never explained the ads angle to me, only that he needed money.

Gabe pressured three of his friends for donations and after picking up the $100, he forgot to get their ad layout (which would have congratulated Gabe for making it into the Texas Cowboys), so it was never published in the ad book.

Gabe's friends told me that he originally felt really proud and honored to be asked to join the Texas Cowboys, especially since he was from Idaho. At first, he was confident that he had made the right decision. Yet later he was so busy doing Cowboy things that his friends saw less and less of him.

Gabe's friend Brian told me that Gabe enjoyed the parties. He liked the Cowboy activities. He was looking forward to going onto the football field to shoot the cannon off at the football games. He liked the whole image. He thought the girls would be impressed and he would brag to his friends about being a Cowboy.

Gabe's phone bill was over $400 before it was disconnected in April for lack of payment. He had also gotten behind on his other bills and was so stressed that he was broken out in pimples and had begun smoking again, a habit he had successfully given up the summer before.

Brian explained to me, "Gabe knew he was going to have to do some work in the Cowboys, selling tickets for the concert and things, but he thought it meant he would have to go an hour or two every day or two to sell ads. He didn't know there would be a quota for it or that there would be punishment for it if he didn't do it."

Brian also told me that Gabe was constantly looking for people to buy ads. Occasionally he would ask people to write a check to the Cowboys and then Gabe would pay them back. Brian said he personally wrote checks "four or five times, usually for $50 or $100."

He added: "Gabe would have people write checks then he'd stop payment. He would pay the fee of $20 that the bank charged to stop payment. He did that a lot. This was going on right up until the end. I wrote a check to the Cowboys and Gabe gave me $200 cash for the check. The check bounced on the day it went through at the bank. After Gabe died, I gave the money to Gabe's roommate for the phone bill.

"Gabe was always worried about the turn-ins. He never said what the penalty would be if he didn't turn in his money. He met most of his turn-ins. Gabe really felt the pressure of turning in his money."

One weekend the Cowboy pledge class was raising money by sponsoring a five Kilometer run. It was a weekend that Crystal was in Austin.

"That morning we waited for a friend and were running late," Crystal told me. "Gabe was scared to death about being late. He said that if he didn't show up on time, that he would have to go through another six to eight weeks of hazing."

After they got there an hour late, Gabe was greatly relieved to find that the pledge trainer was later than he was, which meant that he wouldn't be hazed for his tardiness.

That was the weekend Crystal tried to talk Gabe out of pledging the Cowboys. "This whole thing had become a nightmare," she told me. "He was spending every waking moment that he wasn't in class or studying, knocking on doors to earn money for the Cowboys."

"Give it up," she said to him. "Quit. You don't need to do this."

"I can't," he answered, "I've done too much work already. I've put too much time and money into this. All I have to do now is a couple more weeks and it'll be over."

He told Crystal that he didn't consider that the initiation would be much of an ordeal at all. That's what he had been told by his older Kappa Sig brothers who were Texas Cowboys.

"One weekend we were at a party at the Kappa Sig house," Crystal told me. "Gabe was across the courtyard by the keg with some of his Cowboy brothers [also Kappa Sig brothers] and I watched them. The Cowboys were making him chug beer out of his black felt Cowboy hat. They made him turn the hat inside out and then they were holding it to his face and were using profanities, yelling at him to drink it."

She continued, "Whenever I talked to him, he always told me how miserable and stressed out he was about the Cowboys."

Early in May before she went back to Dallas, she discussed with Gabe when she should come down to see him again. At first, Gabe told her to come down the weekend of the "picnic" (the Cowboy's initiation-picnic), but then changed his mind and said, "No, I don't know what they're going to do to me that weekend. You better come down the weekend before."

"The last time that I saw Gabe," she said, "was the weekend before he died. We went to lunch that Sunday and he said: 'Thank God this is almost over.' He told me that if he had known it was going to be this bad, he would never have joined."

That semester, the Cowboy pledges raised $68,000. Gabe and John's portion of that was $6300, the largest amount any of the two man teams raised that semester.

E-MAILS

The following are excerpts from the e-mails between Gabe and his brother, Brian regarding the Texas Cowboys. I've added my comments in brackets, for clarity.

January 26, 1995, Gabe to his brother Brian:

"This really means nothing to you, but I'll tell you anyway. I got picked to be a Texas Cowboy. It's an organization that raises money for the Texas Association of Retarded People. They only pick three people [two-spring, one-fall] from the big fraternities for the year and a few independents. It is an incredible honor. Kids that go to UT have dreams about being a Cowboy. I really hope you get excited for me because I really want to do this. It's going to take a lot of time and I really want to prove myself. I've never really envisioned myself as being a leader type person and this kind of opportunity will give me a chance to demand the respect and honor that I deserve. As you can probably tell, this is really, REALLY, an incredible honor. I have gotten nothing but congratulations from everyone around me who has knowledge of who the cowboys are. You might know the cowboys as being the guys dressed up like cowboys (hat, boots, chaps, other random shit), who shoot off the cannon when UT scored their points last season-and-every-season-in-football. So after I go through I'll be able to get on TV and shoot a cannon. It's hard to explain it all over e-mail. Try to call me sometime and I'll tell you more about it."

February 8th, Gabe wrote Brian:

"Subject: Cowboy, like the subject: Your brother's a Texas Cowboy. Bet you could put that on your resume and get a job in Texas if you'd like but I've got a feeling you won't be working in Texas anytime soon.

"I'm really stressed out. Turned in 600 dollars for the cowboy thing today and will find out in an hour or two how much I have to turn in next week. It seems strange that I bitch about money so much yet I'm giving an organization thousands of dollars so that I can join. All I have to say is that I'm networking fairly well for a white boy from the middle of Idaho. I was talking to a friend the other day and he said, 'Well shoot, Gabe, if you need some money just call this guy and this guy and come out to lunch with me on Saturday and we'll talk to these guys and … ' … you get the point.

"More important than that though is that about four or five girls loved it after they heard I was going to be a cowboy. stressed. real tired. horny. semi-senile. will call later."

March 10th, Brian e-mailed Gabe:

"hope everything is well in cowboy land."

Gabe responded:

"I'm so sick and tired of it I can't tell you. I've sunk more money into it than I'm willing to tell and all I know is that so far it hasn't been worth it. But supposedly it gets better after you've gone through. Uuuggghhh."

Thursday, April 6th, Gabe wrote:

"Man, I just have no news whatsoever. My life is really getting monotonous right now. I have that cowboys deal going on but that's getting real old and I'm hating it every day I do it. It's kind of like pledgeship in the way that I'm really sick and tired of it, but I'll probably really enjoy it once I get through it. After all the money, time, and effort I've put into it, I better enjoy it.

Write back soon man.

Gabe"

THE TAPPING IN

TEXAS COWBOYS
SILVER SPURS
FEBRUARY 4, 1995

Party after Tap-in Paddling: Kappa Sig brothers. One Cowboy (in center)
Below: Gabe, Taylor & TC Pledge mate John

~5~

PLANNING THE CONCERT AND THE PICNIC

Note: Most of the following information has been taken directly from the statements of the young men who were present at the Texas Cowboys' initiation "picnic."

The Texas Cowboys labeled the officers a little differently, to emulate a ranch with a cowboy setting.

The President was called the Foreman,
The Vice President: the Strawboss,
The Pledge Trainer (Pledge Educator): the Horse Wrangler,
The Treasurer: the Shotgun, and
The Social Chairman: the Camp Cook.

The Executive Council was composed of eight officers: three picnic chairmen who organized the two initiation-picnics each year and three show chairmen, who organized the spring concert and the fall concert. Different chairmen were chosen each semester.

The actives in the Texas Cowboys were called "Oldmen," the pledges "Newmen."

THE OFFICERS
The names of the following five officers have been changed. Their initials are the same.

Carl Branson was the Foreman of the Texas Cowboys the spring semester of 1995. He had been the Pledge Trainer the previous fall of 1994 and on the Executive Council the year before during the fall of 1993 and spring of 1994. He was also on the UT Discipline Policies Committee 1994-1995, and the UT President's Board in 1995. Carl was a senior scheduled to graduate in May of 1995.

Carl had also been the President of the Sigma Alpha Epsilon (SAE) fraternity in 1994 and the State Rush Captain in 1993. The spring semester of 1994 the SAE's were put on probation for a year for hazing due to paddling.

In the spring of 1994 the Texas Cowboys had been charged with hazing due to paddling during the tap-in. They were given a one-year probation penalty through the spring semester of 1995. Probations affected their social calendar and limited their parties with sororities. [1]

Cramer Monroe, the Strawboss (Vice President), was a member of the Fiji fraternity and also a senior scheduled to graduate May 1995. Cramer did not go to the initiation because he had to go to a funeral on Saturday.

Grant Granger was the Horse Wrangler (Pledge Educator/Trainer) of the Texas Cowboys during the 1995 Spring Semester. He had been the Vice President/ Straw Boss for the 1994 Fall Semester, and was Show Chairman during the 1994 Spring Semester. Grant also belonged to the same fraternity as his friend, Carl Branson: the SAE's.

Mike Sagness, a Pi Alpha Phi was the Camp Cook (Social Chairman), and Brick Mickel, a Beta Theta Pi was Shotgun (Treasurer).

WEDNESDAY, APRIL 26, 1995
The Cowboys didn't have a fraternity house, so the Wednesday night pledge meetings were held in the RLM Engineering building on campus.

At the last Wednesday meeting at 6:00 p.m. on April 26th, the Newmen were expected to turn in their money, make preparations for the initiation-picnic and discuss the final details of the Waylon Jennings Concert fundraiser being held by the Cowboys the next evening. They discussed the distribution of wristbands, the sale of concert T-shirts and the pre-concert barbecue. [2, 3, 4, 5]

After the money was turned in at the meeting, all of the twelve officers joined them. Carl explained to them about the concert scheduled the next evening, on Thursday, and the initiation-picnic scheduled for Friday, the following evening. Then they elected the three picnic chairmen from the Executive Council. [5, 6]

The Newmen took a short break while the three newly elected picnic chairs made a list of the supplies they would need for the initiation-picnic. They called the Newmen into the meeting room, answered any questions they had and told them the supplies they were to bring. The Newmen were divided into groups of three, forming nine groups. They were encouraged to be with someone that they didn't previously know. The list of the supplies needed was given to one of the Newmen who distributed a copy to each of the nine groups. [4, 8, 6, 2, 7 & 9]

List of items the Oldmen directed the Newmen to bring to the picnic:

US (Texas Cowboys Oldmen)	THEM (TC Newmen)
20 steaks / Lemon pepper / Seasoning salt	120 Hot dogs / Buns
Charcoal / Lighter fluid/ Matches	60 Bottles of Mad Dog
Hot dogs / Buns	60 Trash bags
Plastic wear / Plates (20) / Cups	25 Cases Pabst
Beans (ranch style)	Wheats [Levis] / Boots Undershirt [optional] White shirt & no lids [hats]
Chips	
Mustard	
Golf balls	One page Essay typed on: "What being a TC has meant"
Football	
Coolers (5) & Ice "*important*"	
Tent – don't buy	
Grill – if they have one	
Premium beer – 15 cases of Bud Light/ Miller Light	
Jim Beam – 2 handles	
Dip / Smokes / Cheaper log of Copenhagen/ Carton Marlboro/ Redman	

PLANNING THE CONCERT AND THE PICNIC 37

At the bottom of the list: "Everything needs to be in boxes. You guys should be at the Delt House at 3:30 p.m. in your wheats and white shirts." [9]

Wheats were the color and name of the Levis that were part of the Newmen uniform. The rest of their uniform was a white, long-sleeved dress shirt, optional undershirt, Cowboy boots and a plain black felt hat.

The only questionable item on the list is the number of bottles of Mad Dog 20/20. The original handwritten list states that 60 bottles of Mad Dog 20/20 were to be purchased. The statements, however, disagreed with that list, and claimed that only 30 bottles were purchased. It's my personal belief that they were asked to bring 60 bottles, which was the actual number taken to the initiation-picnic. (The anonymous letter agreed). [10]

These items are additional items that were brought (or listed for clarity).

4 bags of Charcoal
63 Golf balls, plus another bag full
10 Coolers & 28 bags of Ice
Large pit BBQ grill
25 cases (or more) of Pabst & Shaffer's
15 cases (or more) of Bud Light and Miller Light
Two (1.75) liters of Jim Beam
One (1.75) liters of Jack Daniels
One bottle of Dewar's Scotch
Dip: More than 10 cans of Copenhagen
5 Packs of Red Man Golden Blend "chew"
Sausage, Bacon and Eggs for breakfast (Newmen purchased after they arrived).

After the meeting, the picnic chairmen gave two Newmen money to purchase 30 medium "show" paddles and two large paddles from the Austin Lumber Company. (One statement mentioned there were *five* large paddles purchased). [9,10,11]

Medium "Show" paddles are approximately 22 inches long, 5 inches wide and when referring to paddling someone, they are classified as one-handed paddles. The large paddles are 2 ½ feet long, eight inches wide, requiring both hands for paddling. The large paddles are generally given to the officers. Both types are usually decorated, signed by each member of the pledge class and hung on the wall.

Most of the statements agree there was a total of forty-five cases of beer purchased, which agrees with UT's investigation released by Dr. Sharon Justice from the Dean of Students Office of the University of Texas. That averages one case per person.

You might wonder how 30 young men, all but two of them under the legal drinking age of 21 could purchase so much alcohol. One Newman admitted he used a fake ID card at Sam's club to purchase the liquor he bought. He felt that almost everyone at UT had a fake ID and admitted that he had owned one since he was 16 or 17 years old. For the others, either the liquor stores didn't card them, or, like Gabe, they had a friend purchase the alcohol for them.

THE CONCERT

THURSDAY EVENING, APRIL 27, 1995

Thursday evening the Waylon Jennings concert started at eight o'clock at the Austin City Coliseum. All the Texas Cowboys and their dates had a special room to the side that was connected to a fenced-in area where they enjoyed a catered dinner before the concert started. There were eight kegs of beer.

John Welsh confessed, "It was time to celebrate making it through a rough semester. This was the time to drink. The alcohol flowed."

That night the Cowboys presented $15,000 to the Austin Retarded Citizens School (ARC): money that the pledges had raised.

Crystal, Gabe's girlfriend, couldn't come down from Dallas, so Gabe asked another young lady. The last picture of Gabe was taken that night with his arm around this young lady. He had beer stains down the front of his white, button-down dress shirt, evidence of forced drinking.

PLANNING THE CONCERT AND THE PICNIC

Waylon Jennings Concert
The night before Gabe died
Gabe's shirt has beer stains down the front

~6~

THE INITIATION THEY CALLED "PICNIC"

Formerly called "Hell Night"
Their Story: Taken from the Texas Cowboys' statements

FRIDAY, APRIL 28th, 1995

DRIVING OUT TO THE RANCH, 3:30 – 6:30 p.m.

Twenty-six of the thirty Newmen/ pledges arrived at the Delta Tau Delta fraternity house at 3:30 Friday afternoon, April 28th, the day after the Waylon Jennings concert. One Newman was out of town and never went to the initiation-picnic, and three arrived later in the evening due to work and tests. They were all wearing the Newmen uniform of wheat colored Levis, white dress shirts, and boots. No hats this time.

Gabe's best friend drove him to the Delt fraternity house after they bought three bottles of Mad Dog 20/20.

The group consolidated everything into the largest trucks, maps were distributed, and they were on the road around 4:30 or 5:00 p.m. The ten to twelve cars and trucks caravanned to the Morgan ranch about 30 miles southeast of Austin on the Colorado River. Some of them stopped for gas. Most arrived at the ranch between 6:00 and 6:30 p.m.

The discrepancies in their statements mostly regarded the *timing* of events, probably because some of them, like Gabe, left their watches home.

The map directed them to take the highway to Houston, turning south on one of the county roads to the front gate of the Morgan Ranch.

That area of the country is beautiful, with small rolling hills, not flat like the rest of Texas. It is abundant with beautiful trees, lots of brush and occasional green fields. The front gate was hidden from the county road by thick trees and brush.

Driving through the front gate, one could easily see the ranch house to the left across the field of this 80-acre ranch. The road followed the fence on the left, past some trees, then turned right in front of the ranch house on their left, where they parked.

James Morgan, the owner of the ranch, was a lawyer from Houston and the father of a former Texas Cowboy. This particular Friday night, Mr. and Mrs. Morgan spent the evening in the otherwise vacant ranch house.

After the lawsuit had closed, I called Mr. Morgan and left a message on his answering machine asking if I could possibly go onto his property and walk down to the river where my son died to pay my final respects. The next day I got a phone call from my lawyer saying that my message was not well received, advising me to keep my distance.

Details about the property have been collected from a trip I made to the front gate of the Morgan Ranch two weeks after that phone call. I also used pictures of the ranch provided by Mr. Morgan, plus photos I took from across the river, police notes with maps drawn on them, and descriptions of the ranch from the statements which included maps.

Three Newmen arrived before Foreman Carl Branson got there, at around 5:30 or 6:00 p.m. Carl instructed the three to stand by the front gate and direct the others onto the property.

Before any more arrived, Carl and Horse Wrangler Grant walked up to the front door of the ranch house and introduced themselves to Mr. Morgan, thanking him for allowing them to use the property.

The Cowboys had used the ranch for the past ten years for their initiation-picnics. Mr. Morgan said he was there to advise the group to: (1) Remove all trash, (2) Leave the cars at the house, not at the river (he didn't want them driving over the grass), and (3) to warn them not to go near the river or the cliffs.

While unloading the vehicles, Carl and one of the picnic chairs collected all of the car keys for two reasons: (1) so no one could drive around on the ranch or leave after drinking, and (2) so no one would lose them.

They also gathered up watches, belts, and wallets, bagged them and put them in the back of one of the Oldmen's trucks.

At least nine of the thirty Newmen said they didn't hear Mr. Morgan's warning to stay away from the river, including the carload of guys who stopped to help some lady with a car full of children and a flat tire, and the three guys who were in the first group to arrive. On the other hand, one Newman said he heard the warning fifteen times. This was important because in their interrogatories, they stated that all of the Newmen were told repeatedly about the cliffs and the river.

The Oldmen weren't expected to bring anything, yet some did, like Grant Granger, who brought wood, groceries and beer. Other Oldmen brought blankets, sleeping bags, pillows and chairs and bottles of hard liquor.

None of the Newmen had been told to bring any camping gear, sleeping bags, tents, blankets or similar overnight gear. Most thought they'd be there overnight and that they would be up all night so they wouldn't need bedrolls. One Newman brought a change of clothes; a couple others brought blankets.

Mr. Morgan allowed only four of the vehicles to be driven to the campsites. The rest of them had to remain next to the ranch house. Three trucks and one car were driven down to the Oldmen's campsite and unloaded.

CAMPSITES

There were two separate campsites: one for the Oldmen and one for the Newmen. They were both located a little less than a mile from the ranch house or as one Newman put it, a ten-minute walk.

The Oldmen's campsite was approached by a dirt road, which gently sloped down toward the river. (See Map of Property)

The Newmen's camp was up the hill to the left from the Oldmen's campsite in a grassy clearing, and was a little farther from the river than the Oldmen's camp. Approximately 400 feet apart, neither campsite was visible from the other because the trees and brush on the hillside were so thick and the hill so steep. Earlier that day, Mr. Morgan mowed a path through the brush and trees between the camps.

SETTING UP THE OLDMEN'S CAMP 7:00 - 8:00 p.m.

The Newmen were in charge of setting up both camps. They gathered wood and set up the Oldmen's campfire first. Most of the wood came from a stack of mesquite wood next to the ranch house.

Several Newmen discovered a pavilion they were told they could use if the weather was bad. It was located about halfway to the river from the Newmen's camp. Next to the pavilion was a beautiful grassy area surrounded by trees, overlooking the majestic Colorado River far below. The steep embankment to the river via the pavilion was thick with numerous trees and brush. (See pictures)

When Newman Cliff Condrey first saw the river, he thought it might be fun to go swimming later. One Oldman stated that he had been to many picnics since his in 1993 and that this was the first time he had ever seen the river and didn't even know it was the Colorado.

The Newmen unpacked all the beer at the Oldmen's camp, filling the coolers and icing down the "better beer" (Budweiser, Miller Lite and Bud Lite). They were told it was only for the Oldmen. Under supervision, they stacked the cheaper beer (Pabst and Schaffer) on the ground, not in coolers, setting the Mad Dog 20/20 beside the fire to get warm.

The rest of the food and supplies were unloaded at the Oldmen's camp. They divided up chores, setting up rocks in a circle for the campsite, gathering wood and unloading the heavy BBQ grill beside the campsite. Two brothers set up the tent next to the Oldmen's camp.

Meanwhile Carl and three of the Oldmen began hitting golf balls off a cliff into the river. They had a contest for the longest drive while some of the Newmen watched. (No one asked the Newmen to retrieve the balls from the river.)

Another group began chipping balls into a field going the other direction away from Carl's group. Eventually a few of the Newmen were asked to retrieve some of the balls from the field, an exercise termed "shagging."

Everyone inferred that the atmosphere at that time was fun and relaxed. Those who remained at the campfire were throwing a football around. The Oldmen started drinking as soon as they got there and the Newmen were given permission to begin drinking shortly after they finished setting up both camps.

THE INITIATION THEY CALLED "PICNIC"

Above: Morgan Ranch House
Below: Road around Ranch House toward the river

Above: Newmen's Campsite, trees and bushes in background looking toward Oldmen's campsite
Below: Oldmen's Campsite. River on the left, past trees

THE INITIATION THEY CALLED "PICNIC"

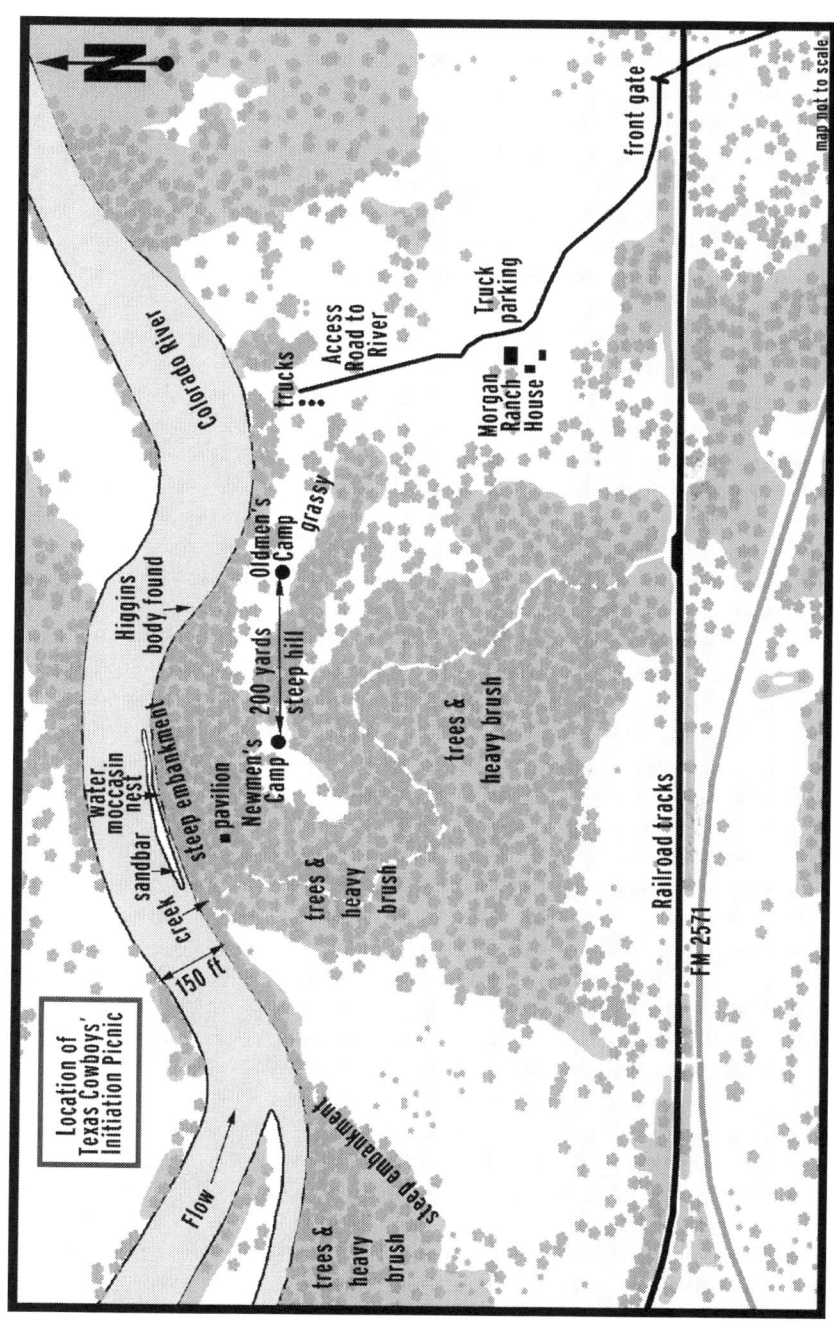

Map of Property

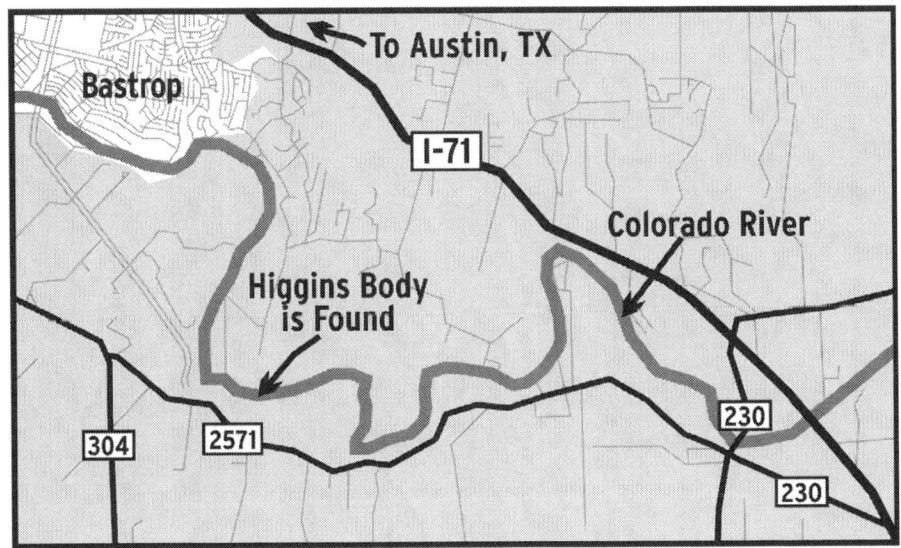

Map of Bastrop

Four of the Newmen were sent into Bastrop to the local HEB grocery store to get some bacon, sausage, and eggs for breakfast and to pick up a bottle of Dewar's Scotch.

SETTING UP THE NEWMEN'S CAMP 8:00 – 9:00 p.m.

After the Oldmen's camp was set up, the three picnic co-chairmen led the Newmen up the hill to show them where their campsite would be. The Newmen dug a hole for the fire, set some rocks in a circle around the hole and collected firewood.

The picnic chairmen started the Newmen's campfire for them and explained to them that they were there to help them and if they had any questions, to ask. When the three were done talking, they "could tell that the Newmen all wanted a beer, so everyone grabbed a beer" and "slammed it together."

After the Newmen's campsite was set up, they were allowed to officially start drinking, though some, like Gabe, had already begun to drink.

Traditionally, all initiation-picnics had two campsites until the next morning when the groups united into one camp. The single campfire ceremony the next morning signified the transition from being a Newman to becoming an Oldman. The concept was that when the

Oldmen felt the Newmen deserved to join them, they were all invited to the Oldmen's campfire to become a part of the organization.

The three picnic chairmen had the Newmen "number off" and divide into groups of three with other Newmen they did not know in an attempt to acquaint them with other guys outside their own fraternity. There were nine groups of three. (These were not the same three man groups that had been selected on Wednesday night). Each group was to stay together and watch out for the other two in their group. This system had always been used in the past.

They were told that if they didn't feel comfortable doing any of the activities, they didn't have to do them, and that they should stay close to the two buddies in their group. It was supposed to be a fun night. They were told there would be no problem with jokes, but were warned, "not to be smart asses."

The picnic chairmen explained the horn honking procedure as follows: One of the trucks beside the Oldmen's campsite would honk a certain number of times, to call each group down. For instance, one horn honk was for group one, two honks was for group two, three honks for group three. One long honk meant the Newmen were to all go down together. They were told that as soon as they heard the horn honks, the group that was called should immediately run down the hill.

The three picnic chairmen asked Gabe and John Welsh to accompany them down the hill to the Oldmen's camp. Gabe and John were introduced to all the Oldmen who congratulated them for being the two who raised the most money. They were asked to help cook. On the flip side, one Oldman said he didn't know who Gabe was, had never met him and probably couldn't pick him out of a group.

It was dark by the time both camps were set up. The Newmen were all gathered around their campfire enjoying each other, telling jokes and talking while waiting to be called down to the Oldmen's campfire.

Carl, Grant, and some other officers walked up the hill before everything started, to congratulate the Newmen for raising money for the Cowboys and making it through the semester.

"This is it!" They said, "You've done a good job! You won't regret coming to the picnic! In the morning you will be glad you were here and hadn't missed it." The officers encouraged them to stay involved at the Rosedale School then shared what the Texas Cowboys organization meant to them, what ideas they had for the future and some of the history of the Cowboys. Then the group of Oldmen walked back down the hill.

EATING AND DRINKING 9:00 – 11:00 p.m.

The Newmen were sitting around their campfire when out of the silence of the dark night they heard the first truck horn honking. A few seconds of hush fell over the group as they all listened. Only one honk! Group #1 took off running down the hill!

"My group was summoned first," one Newman wrote in his statement. "We were told to dig a trench around the Oldmen's campfire and set up the BBQ grill with coals. When we finished, we were offered a beer and since it was Bud or Bud Lite rather than the crummy brands at our camp [that were warm], we took the beer that was offered. We returned 5 to 10 minutes later and told the others: 'It was nothing! We just talked and drank with the Oldmen.'"

Horse Wrangler Grant Granger began cooking steaks for the officers on the large BBQ grill. Two other Oldmen joined him, cooking at least three batches of steaks and heating up beans for the Oldmen. Then they started cooking hot dogs for the Newmen.

Group one arrived back at the Newmen's camp just as the horn honked two times. Group #2 jumped up and ran down the hill. They returned a short time later with hot dogs, buns and chips to share with the group. The horn honked three times. Group #3 took off running. And so on.

Sometime around 9:30 p.m., two sets of Oldmen left the group to wait at the front gate of the ranch for the Newmen who were coming late. Both sets of Oldmen waited for a while for the Newmen to arrive, which didn't happen, so they returned to the campsite. Both Newmen arrived a couple hours later.

As each group of Newmen were called down, the Oldmen sat around their campfire eating their steaks and drinking, "having a good time."

Most groups stayed only about ten minutes at the Oldmen's camp, drank beer, visited, ate hot dogs and chips, helped stoke the fire or cook, then returned back to their camp. When each group of Newmen left the officers' camp, they took hot dogs, buns, and chips back to share with the others.

Several Newmen commented that they helped carry eight to ten cases of beer back to their camp and that, at one point there were 18 cases of beer at the Newmen's campsite. The beer was warm, but "everyone had a beer in hand."

Groups one through six were called a minimum of two to four times each. Group two was called down at least six or seven times, and groups 7, 8, and 9 were not called down at all.

Cliff Condrey who was in group nine with Gabe and Todd Kinsel thought that the reason why they weren't called down was because the Oldmen must have gotten tired of honking the horn so many times!

The instructions about the horn honkings had been obviously a little confusing. Some thought that each additional horn honk meant that the next group should go down. Some thought that each honk designated the number of the group to go down. Amidst the noise and the excitement of the evening, the instructions were long gone and no one seemed to mind. They were just all having fun.

President Carl Branson's statement said that there wasn't much drinking at all and that he "didn't see any of the [Newmen] chug beers or be asked to do so." Yet in the statements, several Newmen said they were asked to "chug a beer" and that there was more than one beer chugging contest. Many were asked to "grab a beer," and were glad to do so, since the beer that was offered them was cold and better tasting.

One Oldman said, "After several beers, I began to drink Jim Beam and cokes. When the steaks were ready, I ate two of them and continued to drink. Soon after eating, I began to feel sick, vomited, and went to sleep in the back of someone's car."

COPENHAGEN TOBACCO Approximately 9:30 – 10:30 p.m.

Carl took over cooking the hot dogs and asked another Cowboy to bring him a can of Copenhagen chewing tobacco. He cooked a few hot dogs, sprinkled Copenhagen on them, then asked one of the picnic chairmen to take over cooking. At least seven hot dogs were laced with Copenhagen: five to Newmen and two to Oldmen who were supposedly "tricked into eating one."

Their justification for the Copenhagen on the hot dogs was that there were Newmen who had been sneaking down to the Oldmen's camp, stealing their hats and beer, admittedly encouraged in these pranks. In return, the Oldmen felt they were obliged to feed them hotdogs laced with Copenhagen.

"My [hot dog] had beans, onions, and some Copenhagen," confessed one Newman. He added, "One of the Oldmen took and threw it on the fire, and said, 'You can't eat that.' I think it was [Carl Branson] the President. He brought me another one, a good one."

Pledge trainer Grant Granger, one of the two main cooks, said in his statement that he was not aware of anyone getting a hot dog with Copenhagen on it.

ROUGH HOUSING & PRANKS Around 10:00 – 11:00 p.m.

From the time they pulled onto the Morgan Ranch, the Newmen had been encouraged to play pranks, specifically to steal hats from the Oldmen. They willingly obliged and at least five of the Newmen managed to steal baseball hats off the heads of the Oldmen by running into their camp and quickly fleeing without getting caught. Occasionally a cold beer was successfully confiscated, a delightful feat.

The Oldmen labeled Newman Cliff Condrey the "head stealer" because he had successfully swiped the hats off two of the Oldmen and heisted beer from beside the Oldmen's campfire.

It was a moonless night and the trail down the hill to the Oldmen's camp was very dark. The only light was an occasional flicker from the Oldmen's campfire. Barely able to see the trees and bushes as they ran down the hill, they found they couldn't run as fast as they wanted. Some were able to see a little better by following the white shirts of the ones in front of them.

After the Oldmen finished eating, the three in charge of the horn honking positioned two trucks to shine their headlights on the path where the Newmen would be running down the hill. The remaining Oldmen hid behind the trees and bushes toward the bottom of the hill.

The Newmen were sitting around their campfire when they heard one long horn honk. They immediately all took off running down the hill going lickety-split, since for the first time they could actually see what was in front of them, thanks to the headlights shining on the path. Prime candidates, most were successfully ambushed and tackled with hardly any effort.

TESTIMONIALS 10:30 p.m. – 12:00 Midnight

Someone yelled that they were about to read the testimonials. These were the one-page essays the Newmen were asked to bring to the initiation-picnic, stating why they wanted to be a Texas Cowboy. Several guys took off running for the trucks next to the ranch house to retrieve their essays. No one in Gabe's group wanted to run that far, so they chose to "wing it," leaving their essays in their truck.

Carl had gathered most of the testimonials earlier and began handing them back. All forty-three guys (27 Newmen and 16 Oldmen) now circled around the Oldmen's campfire. One at a time each Newman was invited to stand in front of the others and with the aid of Carl's flashlight, read his own testimonial about what he thought it meant to be a Texas Cowboy.

They talked about the work they had done during the semester at the Austin Retarded Citizens School (The ARC, also called the Rosedale School), and how they wanted to be involved in the future. Those who didn't have their testimonials with them, like Gabe's group, waited until the others were done speaking to share their thoughts. Each one thanked the others and when they were finished, everyone clapped.

While the testimonials were read, two of the Oldmen continued to cook hot dogs for the Newmen who were still hungry.

Two Newmen arrived late. One grabbed a hot dog, sat down and waited for his turn. He was the last Newman to share his thoughts and when he finished, several Oldmen got up, one at a time and spoke about what it meant to be a Cowboy.

The Oldmen congratulated them for a successful show and fundraising. They mentioned how "moving" the previous evening had been when Carl had presented the check of $15,000 to the ARC.

The officers talked about how the Cowboys were an honorary service organization and not an honorary *volunteer* service organization. This meant that they should continue their work in serving others even after they were Oldmen. They mentioned that the initiation-picnic was a fun time where they would be together as a group for the last time since it was the end of the semester, and that they should take advantage of the opportunity to get to know one another better.

This was when Newman John Welsh noticed that during their speeches, the Oldmen were being redundant, talking in a monotone. John thought to himself: *"They've been drinking for a while."* His statement said: "Everyone was drinking. They were not all completely drunk but some may have been."

Most of the Newmen felt that reading the testimonials was solemn and meaningful and the most important part of the entire night. One considered it to be the defining point of the evening. Another said that he had not felt like a member of the Cowboys until that point.

Solemn or not, the drinking continued. One Newman wrote: "I guess I had quite a few beers by this time. I know I was drinking pretty steady. It was late. I don't think I was very drunk yet. I had been drinking though."

The Newmen went back up to their campfire, hung out, drank beer, and talked, giving each other "high-five's." Happy to be finished, they all told stories and jokes, exchanged hugs and ate hot dogs, cooked or not.

MAD DOG DRINKING RACES Midnight to 12:30 a.m.

Once again, the familiar long honk was heard in the distance. All the Newmen jumped up and ran down the hill together

The ground was covered with empty beer cans. Most Newmen had consumed 8-12 beers by this time; many of the Oldmen drank mixed drinks, some, both beer and hard liquor.

No one really knows how the races got started. After the Newmen reached the Oldmen's camp, the warmed bottles of Mad Dog 20/20 were retrieved from beside the Oldmen's campfire and taken to the clearing several feet away.

Mad Dog 20/20 is an extremely sweet, cheap wine, labeled: "the dregs of the barrel." It would be a fitting drink if the objective were to make you sick and vomit. In this case, that was the objective.

Without any sign of instruction, everyone just grabbed a bottle of Mad Dog and the entire group went out of control, yelling and wildly drinking, randomly racing against each other. In the noise and chaos, some were chugging one-on-one, some group-on-group, in threes. A few Oldmen joined in the race, grabbing beers instead of Mad Dog.

Eventually, they got a little more organized and the Newmen were grouped into groups of three, kneeling on one or both knees, positioned and ready to race.

Everyone was cheering and yelling: "Go!" or "Drink it!"

Some of the Oldmen stood behind their younger fraternity brothers and told them to pour their Mad Dog out on the ground and not drink it. In the darkness no one noticed. Some were told to make it look like they had spilled it on their shirts while chugging.

There were Newmen who finished drinking the Mad Dog with ease and some who had great difficulty. Some were really gung-ho and drank the whole bottle, like Gabe, who had no one standing behind him coaching him not to. It was a fraternity thing and no one from his fraternity was present.

Most Newmen were either pouring a lot of their Mad Dog out before they raced or simply not finishing them. One Newman thought his friend was a wimp because he poured out half his bottle before racing.

Standing on the sidelines watching it all, some of the Oldmen would select whomever they wanted to win each race, and then root for them. One admitted that he felt they just wanted the Newmen they were rooting for to win, even if it meant having him pour three-fourths of his bottle out in order to do so.

Newmen were getting sick and vomiting "because it was so sweet." One said he thought the whole Mad Dog thing was to control the drinking because it made you vomit what you'd already drunk, to get it out of your system.

Though Gabe drank most of his Mad Dog, he didn't appear to have any difficulty standing, walking, or talking afterwards, nor did he up-chuck any of it.

No one seemed to be in charge of this event and not everyone seemed to be involved. A couple of the guys felt sick and were hung over from the night before so they weren't drinking much. The statements claimed that no one was punished, reprimanded or criticized for not drinking, and no one was forced to drink the Mad Dog 20/20, nor were they threatened if they didn't want to. The race was not considered to be a big deal since no winners were recognized. One Newman did not participate at all because he had an ulcer and was excused from any of the drinking activities.

A number of the Oldmen were just standing around visiting, laughing and drinking beer. Some were throwing a football [in the dark?!]; others were eating hot dogs. Most of the Oldmen retreated to their campfire and just "hung out" away from the noise.

Having passed out on the grass, one Newman "came to" and was told to go back up to the Newmen's camp. He did, and the next time he woke up, it was daylight.

The Newmen did not return to their camp after the Mad Dog 20/20 races but remained down at the Oldmen's camp for the next event.

MONKEY ROLLS Approximately 12:30 – 1:00 a.m.

Pledge trainer Grant Granger told the Newmen to line up and instructed them how to do monkey rolls, a drill from high school football. Also called a three-man weave, three guys were to get on all fours side-by-side then one at a time they were to jump over the other two in a quickened pace. It was a traditional thing they did at the initiation-picnic, and some believed that it gave them a sense of camaraderie.

Monkey rolls are hard to do even sober without falling down. Each group did the exercise until someone messed up and they fell on each other. Most weren't able to do it very long. The Oldmen thought it was funny to watch the Newmen in their drunken state. Most of them were laughing and cheering them on, very entertained.

After everyone had participated, an all-star team was chosen and asked to do the drills a second time because they had survived the longest. That three-man team was Gabe's group, including Cliff Condrey and Todd Shapiro.

They ran through the drill and a worn out Gabe walked up to the place where John Welsh was sitting, going "from standing to sitting in one motion like drunk people do," John related in his statement. He felt that Gabe could handle his liquor because he had seen Gabe drink beer for two to three hours then put on his knee brace and shorts and play basketball for two hours at the fraternity house.

John was sure Gabe had been drinking but wasn't sure how much, so he asked Gabe, "Are you okay?"

Gabe replied, "Yeah, I'm fine."

"You don't look fine to me, you look peaked," John told him. He felt that Gabe was not paying attention to him so he slapped him around and told him, "You may say you are fine, but if the wine bites you in the butt thirty minutes from now I don't care whether you are in my group or not. You tell me and I will take care of you."

Cliff and Todd, both tall, strong athletes, were so worn out from the monkey rolls, they crashed on the ground.

BACK TO THEIR CAMPSITE Around 1:00 – 2:30 a.m.
Around fifteen minutes after the monkey rolls were finished the Newmen were told to go back up to their campfire and go to sleep: the activities were over for the night. According to most, it was sometime around 1:30 or 2:00 in the morning, but even that was a guess-estimate since none of them had watches. Some of them grabbed a hot dog before "staggering up the hill" to their campfire to go to sleep, happy that the initiation really was a "piece of cake" picnic after all.

THE SWAT – Approximately 1:30 – 2:30 a.m.
Mr. Pied Piper, Cliff Condrey, claimed that it was around 2:30 a.m. when they were instructed to return to their campfire. Cliff said he had a watch in his pocket. He and some other Newmen hung back about 20 yards from the Oldmen's campfire, hoping to steal a cooler of beer from the Oldmen, but it didn't work out. Instead, Cliff ran through their campsite as a joke and (again) swiped one of the Oldmen's cowboy hats.

Having no clue who it was in the dark, several Oldmen jumped up and "chased the thief until they finally caught him." They took Condrey back to the Oldmen's camp and discussed with the others what they should do with him, deciding they would give him a swat for taking the Oldman's hat. They did and he was paddled once.

The Oldman who had gotten sick earlier and fallen asleep in the back of someone's car, awakened to find the group gathered around the campfire. A few Newmen were with them, [probably Cliff and friends], horsing around and wrestling with one another.

Cliff and the other Newmen returned to their campfire. According to the statements, the paddling precipitated a half hour discussion among the Oldmen as to whether or not they should "swat" the Newman. Some thought it was not a big deal and that they should give the Newman "something to remember about this special night."

Carl's statement says that he took the initiative and decided against the paddling, since he was the foreman. There was no further discussion about it. They resumed "lighthearted conversation and story-telling" around the Oldmen's fire.

COMMENTS

It didn't make much sense to me that they would be sitting around for a half hour (or longer), discussing "whether or not they should administer one swat" when it had already been administered! Then Carl, the Cowboys' Foreman, decided against it: *after* the fact?

The discussion about one swat seemed even more trivial after finding out what the Texas Cowboys had planned for the Newmen the following morning, in the name of "tradition."

THE INITIATION THEY CALLED "PICNIC"

Above: View of where the boys entered into the woods to the river
Below: View where the boys entered the creek
The shore drops off sharply several feet to the river on the left

Above: Looking toward the Colorado River at the mouth of the creek
Below: Looking across river from Morgan's property.
This is down river from the sandbars
River current moves left to right, East to West, looking North

~7~

TO THE RIVER

Because of the discrepancies *of the statements, the timing of this event could have been anywhere between* 1:00–3:00 *a.m.*

Sitting around the fire, drinking and talking, the Newmen thought they were done for the night. They were excited that they had finished a semester of hard work and that they were so close to becoming coveted "Texas Cowboys." There was a lot of playing around, congratulating one another, storytelling and "having a good time."

Six of the Newmen took off to go to the pavilion to sleep on the cement, even though they had no bedrolls, pillows or blankets. Most of the guys remained beside the campfire and fell asleep.

COMMENTS

Until this point, their stories were entirely believable, though I questioned some minor things. For instance, the statement: "no one was forced to drink" infers that through the evening, though everyone was drinking, there was no pressure on any of them to drink. This disallows that element of peer pressure, which was present.

It has been from this point on that I have questioned the truthfulness of their stories. There are a variety of reasons for those conclusions, which will be discussed in a later chapter. In order to lay the groundwork of that chapter, the following section has been taken from their statements to present what *they said* happened.

TO THE RIVER

The Newmen weren't at their camp very long before Cliff suggested to Todd and Gabe that they go swimming. Group nine, the all-star trio, winners of the Monkey Roll three-man-weave contest, composed of Cliff, Gabe, and Todd, led the way. The others followed.

John Welsh's statement said that everyone was all "liquored up," so their response was: "Yea, it's a great idea." He reasoned, "It was the typical college, invincible, fun, great thing to do."

"Gabe Higgins was sitting next to me," Matt's statement said, "and he got up and left to go down to the river. I was pretty sober, and I was unsure as to whether or not to go, because it was cold, and it really didn't sound like that good of an idea. Gabe was pretty 'messed up,' meaning that he was drunk. His speech wasn't slurred, and he wasn't staggering, but I thought that he was pretty drunk, judging from his eyes. After Gabe left me at the campfire, I never saw him again. I decided to go to the river, because I felt like everybody was going to go."

The group started toward the pavilion. The half dozen who were already at the pavilion heard the main group coming through the woods. They were going to hide in the bushes and jump out and scare them but they didn't act quickly enough. The two groups joined and they all headed down to the river.

A couple of guys who started out in the main group had second thoughts about going to the river. They lagged behind, ready to go back to the campfire then changed their minds and caught up with the group.

Eight of the twenty-nine stayed behind at the campfire. Three of the eight changed their minds and caught up with the main group. Five remained at the campfire: One had passed out earlier and the remaining four were asleep, thinking it was a foolish thing to do or they just didn't want to get wet.

Even some who went to the river admitted that they thought it wasn't a smart thing to do, but they did it anyway because everybody else was going.

Without flashlights it took fifteen minutes or longer for them to get down to the river "because it was dark and there was no moonlight." Away from the campfire they could only see three to four feet in front of them at best. The pitch-black night seemed to swallow them up as they stumbled through the treacherous underbrush, tripping over the barbed wire, old tree stumps and uneven ground.

It became evident that to keep from falling, they had to hold hands, link arms, or hold the belt loops of the person in front of them. Even walking slowly, they'd look out for each other and if one tripped on a tree stump (which happened), they'd yell, "Tree stump here!"

One pledge turned to another and commented: "Man, this is dangerous!"

Two separate groups reached the river, a few minutes apart.

As they each came to the steep slope that led down to the creek, they formed a human chain, holding onto each other. This obviously didn't work for everybody, because some of them fell down into the creek. Others jumped.

Cliff slipped as he edged his way down the steep embankment. Gabe caught him and they helped each other into the creek.

ON THE RIVER Between 2:00 – 3:00 a.m.

The Texas Rangers' report mentioned that the creek that led into the river was about twenty feet across and up to four feet deep. They waded through the knee-deep part of the creek and into the Colorado River where it was thigh-deep, possibly hip-deep water to a sandbar about a fourth of the way out into the Colorado River. The Texas Rangers' Report said the water was about 70 degrees.

The rocky creek and river bottom required them to keep their boots on. No one took off any Levis, though a few shirts came off. Most had absolutely no desire to swim so they stayed on the sandbar, like the Newman who realized he was "legally drunk." Plus he had eaten a hot dog with Copenhagen earlier, which upset his stomach and made him throw up.

There were actually two sandbars, the smaller one being a couple steps downstream from where they were. Once they were there they began "high-five-ing" and congratulating each other, elated that they were done with the initiation and had made it this far. The whooping and hollering became horseplay and throwing each other around. Then it became more serious wrestling and fighting.

Newman Patrick H. told the police later, "We got to the sandbar and started splashing around, wrestling with each other. At one point Gabe and I were wrestling; he grabbed my shirt and I pulled away. When I did that, my shirt got ripped. I didn't see him after that." A later interview with Patrick clarified that Gabe had ripped Patrick's *undershirt* while fighting in the knee-deep water close to the sandbar.

Gabe wrestled with another (nameless) Newman in the knee-deep water, a confession made by the Newman who pulled them apart.

It was dark and foggy, overcast with no moon. They couldn't make out individual faces, yet they could see each other close up, possibly because they were all wearing white shirts. The water didn't appear to be too cold.

What the Cowboy initiates *didn't* know was that there was a water moccasin nest hidden in the elbow of shallow water between the sandbar and the Morgan Ranch.

SWIMMING Sometime between 2:00 – 3:00 a.m.

The river was very wide. One Newmen estimated that he thought it was approximately 50 yards wide. Past the sandbar, the river quickly got deep with a swift current. The opposite bank was approximately 8-10 feet deep.

Referring to the current, one commented: "It was real dangerous." Someone else said that he never felt a current and that he couldn't believe that Gabe had drowned.

The first group of four Newmen swam across the river. As they approached the other shore, one of them, Todd S. (not the one in Gabe's group), got tired of swimming, so he asked the guy just ahead of him to help him. He was pulled to a tree branch where he held on and rested. The bank was too steep to climb up. On the way back, Todd again felt that he couldn't make it all the way.

"Help me! Somebody help me!" he hollered. At that moment, the guy in front of him reached the sandbar, turning around to see Cliff, closest to Todd, dive under him and push him forward until Todd felt the sandbar under his feet.

They were probably in the water around 15 to 30 minutes.

Cliff's commented: "I didn't see Gabe. The last time I saw [him] or could say I had eye contact with Gabe was when we first went in the water" at the creek.

John Welsh, Gabe's pledge mate, was one of the last ones to get to the river. He said he never saw Gabe on the river that night.

THE OLDMEN Sometime between 2:00 – 3:00 a.m.

At the Oldmen's camp they were still sitting around drinking.

"I heard voices down by the river," Jimmy's statement says. "Steve and I jumped up with a flashlight and [ran] down to the river to see what was happening." When they got there, they saw several of the Newmen swimming and wading.

Jimmy "angrily" screamed at them: "Get out of the water!"

Steve also yelled, "What do you think you're doing?"

"Fuck you," the Newmen yelled back.

Jimmy ran back to the Oldmen's campfire and told them what had happened.

Most of the Oldmen jumped up and ran back to the river with Jimmy, all of them yelling to the Newmen to get out of the water, and "Get back to your camp fast."

In the distance they could hear one long horn honk calling the Newmen to the Oldmen's campfire. It only caused more confusion. It startled and awakened the handful of Newmen who were asleep at their campfire. It was a declaration that ordered them to run down to the Oldmen's camp. They didn't know what was going on but quickly decided they weren't going anywhere without the others. When they didn't go, some of the Oldmen stormed up to their camp to get them.

Jimmy was one of the Oldmen who ran up the hill to the Newmen's campfire. He was extremely agitated, "livid," yelling: "Where are the other Newmen? Run down to the river and help the other Newmen get back! You have five minutes to get your brothers out of the water!" No one moved. He added: "They could have drowned!"

Frustrated and tired, one Newman got up, walked out of sight and sat down. Then the Oldmen left.

The Oldmen were yanking guys out and pushing them up the cliff. Some of the Newmen locked arms and climbed up the steep embankment. They were slipping all over the place. Everyone was yelling.

The uphill walk to the Newmen's camp was much easier because they didn't have to "link up" by holding onto each other's belt loops and they could see the path a little better due to a few flashlights. The group was making tons of noise, yelling and hollering.

Newman Sean was the last one out of the river. He turned to look back one last time: "I could not see anyone behind me. I felt completely sober at this point. There was no significant moon. I definitely remember that I looked back and looked to the bank on the other side and I could not see any heads at the embankment. The river was peaceful. It was not a roaring river; it was quiet, gently moving, not fast: a lazy river."

Not quite in sync with things, one Oldman stated: "Around 2:30 a.m. I was about to go to sleep and I decided to walk up to the Newmen's campsite and just say goodnight and see what they were doing. When I arrived, the place was in disarray. People were yelling and screaming and most of the Newmen were fully dressed and soaking wet."

Newmen John Welsh, Gabe's pledge mate, and their friend, Newman Todd Kinsel (who had won the Monkey Rolls with Gabe, not the same Todd from the river) walked together coming back from the river. They each knew immediately that Gabe was not with them. They were upset at the time that was wasted.

When the group reached the Newmen's camp, they didn't immediately "circle up," which was what John and Todd assumed they would do. Carl and Grant were mad because the Newmen had gone down to the river after being told not to. Grant was mad about anyone yelling "fuck off" and was trying to figure out who said it. "There should be respect" among the guys, he said.

When the Newmen expressed concern about Gabe, Carl responded: "Relax, we've got people looking for him." Grant said they were not terribly worried at first, even after the head count, because they heard Gabe had not been swimming across the river.

"The Oldmen spent about five minutes talking about respecting their wishes" and reminding us "not to go in the river," John Welsh's statement said. Todd K. yelled "We get the point, let's find him right now."

Newman Patrick H. (the one that tore Gabe's shirt) was the last one to get back to the campfire and when he got there, he observed everyone sitting around the fire as the Oldmen were talking about how great it was to meet guys from different fraternities and what "Cowboys" is all about.

The Newmen finally "circled up" and a head count was taken. They counted off.

There were 28 pledges.

One was missing.

~8~

THE SEARCH BEGINS

SATURDAY MORNING, APRIL 29, 1995
Approximately 3:00 – 5:00 a.m.

One statement declared that someone (no name was given) said: "I'll kill him when he gets back," because "Higgins had really put [us] out and this was certainly not the way the picnic had been planned to go."

It was around 3:00 a.m. when they counted off at the Newmen's camp. Total mayhem set in. Lots of noise. Chaos. Yelling. Oldmen going in every which direction.

The Oldmen told the Newmen to "stay put" at their campfire because they didn't want anyone else lost in the woods. They also told them not to worry – that Gabe had probably just wandered off and had passed out or was sleeping against a tree. They were also told to get some sleep, while the Oldmen looked for Gabe.

Several Newmen wanted to help look for Gabe, voicing their desire to do so, but the Oldmen told them that they didn't want to jeopardize anyone else getting lost or hurt, so only the guys who didn't drink much were asked to search. Eventually, more of the Newmen joined in the search.

Newman Cliff Condrey was asked to lead the Oldmen on the exact path that the Newmen had taken to and from the river. Carl Branson, Cliff and Oldman Jason Hicks walked along the path calling Gabe's name continuously. When they got to the river, Carl and Cliff got into the water while Jason went back up the path calling Gabe's name.

Carl and Cliff swam to the other side and back, crossing the sandbar, walking through the woods and meeting up with Grant and the others who had been searching through the woods with flashlights. Cliff and Grant then swam across the river, coming back through the wooded area, all the time calling out Gabe's name.

Two other officers did practically the same thing, stripping to their boxers, wading and swimming across the river looking for Gabe, repeatedly calling Gabe's name. Others eventually joined in swimming across the river and searching the riverbanks.

It was so dark and the visibility so bad that a few of them drove their trucks up to the Newmen's campsite, then into the grassy field overlooking the river to shine their lights onto the river.

Several others went down to the river with flashlights to continue the search with Carl and Grant. They looked together in groups and individually, through the woods, along the riverbank, between the camps, at the creek bed and the inclines, and along the sandbar and the other side of the river.

It was "pitch dark" and most of them thought Gabe had fallen asleep somewhere, that he was on the other side of the river, or had gotten lost. Some got discouraged after an hour or so and went back to the fire, had another beer and talked to the guys.

Some thought Gabe might have been hiding or was playing a prank on them. The Oldmen were not too alarmed and told the Newmen that it had happened in the past that a Newman had fallen asleep or passed out in the woods somewhere. "They weren't very concerned."

John Welsh was deeply concerned and speculated to the others that maybe he'd fallen and broken a leg or broken his ribs and couldn't walk back. Maybe he swam to the wrong bank and become disoriented and was walking in the wrong direction. Maybe he was so fatigued he had passed out. Maybe he walked to the main road, found the nearest convenience store, a 3-4 mile walk, and called someone to pick him up. "There still seemed possibilities."

At the oldmen's fire, they were joking around. The group was not somber; it was "party-party." It did not cross their minds that anything was seriously wrong. Some thought Gabe was on the other side of the river, possibly lost on one of the other ranches, or on the road, but certainly not in the river.

It was late and entirely too dark to see. They searched the river until the current felt significantly stronger to the point that it might have endangered someone's life to continue. After searching for an hour or two, they decided to discontinue the search and wait until sunrise. Carl walked up the hill and told the Newmen.

Those who were wet from swimming stood by the fire to dry themselves. Those who spent time in the water, like Cliff Condrey and Jimmy Lederer, worn out from looking, collapsed and fell asleep: Cliff at the Newmen's campfire and Jimmy in his car. Others fell asleep on the ground by the campfire or in their vehicles.

Many of the Newmen went to the pavilion to sleep, though most of them didn't sleep well. It began to rain and thunder. When morning came, it was still drizzling.

THE SEARCH CONTINUES 6:30 a.m. – 12:00 Noon

One-by-one, at the first sign of light, they woke up and began searching in groups of two or more, combing through the woods and calling Gabe's name. They checked the banks of the river and combed through the woods. Between searches, they congregated back at the campfire.

"From sunrise until about 10:00 a.m., we checked every clump of grass, crossing the river back and forth," John Welsh wrote. "Higgins very easily could have said, 'I'll crash here where it's nice and quiet.' The assumption was that Gabe was tired and had found a comfortable spot and fallen asleep."

"When I woke up, everyone else was very solemn," Jimmy Lederer.

Five guys found a shallow point farther down river from the sandbars, which enabled them to walk across to the other side to search. They walked up and down both sides of the river. They searched the edge of the neighboring ranch yelling his name, then regrouping at the campfire and heading out again. "No one considered something was wrong with him."

One pledge speculated: "Up until morning, there were two possibilities: either Gabe had wandered off or he had drowned. When he didn't come back, that's when it really kicked in that something was wrong. Those who were not worried the night before began to worry a little more now."

"I started thinking that it was more serious at about 9:00 – 9:30 a.m.," one Oldman stated. "The fact that he may have drowned didn't hit me until the Sheriff put the boat in the water."

Cell phones were used to call friends in Austin to see if Gabe had somehow made it back there. Carl called his dad, a lawyer in Houston and informed him of the possibility of a potentially serious situation. Lt. Campos, the investigating officer, told me later that he believed that it was early morning when Carl called his father.

John Welsh called the Kappa Sig House and talked to one of the Kappa Sig/ Texas Cowboys. They conducted a search of the fraternity house. Carloads of Cowboys drove out to the ranch to offer help.

When the first group of Oldmen that arrived from Austin got there at about 10:00 p.m., everyone was sitting around and joking about Gabe. Three Oldmen were cooking breakfast. They were telling stories about other guys falling asleep in the bushes, or falling asleep in their cars. Some even thought Gabe had possibly hitched a ride and gone home to go to sleep. Or he could have passed out in the woods somewhere.

One group at 10:30 p.m. was shocked to see several wet and dirty young men about to make their fourth search of the morning.

They started cleaning up the badly trashed campsites, picking up and bagging more trash each time they returned from searching. They loaded it into the back of an Oldman's truck.

A few guys were drinking some of the beer that was left. Everyone sat around the Oldmen's campfire trying to cheer each other up. Some of them were anxious to go to the chili cook off back in Austin and were hoping that Gabe would be found so they could get going.

CALLING THE AUTHORITIES 11:42 a.m.

By 10:45 a.m. everyone began to lose hope. Carl and three of the officers quietly discussed the fact that if Gabe had passed out or was lost, he would have found his way back by now. They decided that they had done all that they could do and it was time to notify Mr. Morgan and the authorities.

Sometime after 11:00 a.m., "Grant, Brick and I went up to the ranch house and talked to Mr. Morgan," Carl's statement read. "He said he would call the Sheriff's office in Bastrop." According to the police log, the phone call was made at 11:42 a.m. Saturday morning.

At noon before the police arrived, two Cowboys frantically made one last effort, wading across the shallow part of the river once more, looking again on the other side for Gabe.

The police arrived at 12:31 p.m. and found everything "meticulously clean." Cpl. Earl Pence's report states: "There was nothing laying around. It was policed pretty good." Lt. Campos' investigation notes state that when they arrived, "There were boys running around swimming the river, dirty, muddy, panicked and looking for Gabe."

Deputy Sheriff Nelson walked to the pavilion and then to the Oldmen's camp talking with Carl, Grant, and Newman Cliff Condrey. He wanted to meet with the young men who saw Gabe last.

"I was so tired it was hard to gauge time by now," Newman Sean said.

THE PADDLES

There were thirty small ceremonial-like "show" paddles and somewhere between two to five big paddles, purchased from the Austin Lumber Company. The small ones were traditionally thrown into the fire to scorch them, then used in the final ceremony where they were hit together in unison. At the end of the initiation they would have been given to the Newmen.

That morning after the authorities had been called, someone suggested that they needed to get rid of the paddles. Earlier, they had been put into one of the cars to protect them from the rain. Someone loaded them up into a truck and began to drive them off the ranch when the ranch owner stopped them and asked them not to leave until the authorities arrived. The truck turned around and returned to the campsite. They left much later and were never questioned about the paddles.

No one reported what happened to the paddles. In the chaos of everything, the Newmen were never given any paddles or documents decreeing that they had passed the initiation or that they had even become Texas Cowboys.

THE RESCUE EFFORTS 12:00 Noon – 4:30 p.m.

They had not been expected to be there past noon, so Mrs. Morgan brought food and water down for everyone. No one was supposed to leave because the police wanted to talk to everyone.

About 12:30 p.m., some of the Newmen tried to leave because they had to go to work (different group from the truck with paddles). They were stopped by Mr. Morgan who asked them to wait until the authorities got there. They waited until the deputy sheriff drove past them, then left. They figured the authorities didn't want to talk to them.

The deputies arrived at the campsite at 12:41 p.m.

Around 1:00 p.m., several of the Cowboys and Newmen received permission from the police officers to leave because they had work or other obligations. It became chaotic and more of them requested to leave.

By 2:00 p.m., they were told they could all leave and almost everyone went home. One Newman admitted that he left because he didn't want to be there when they found Gabe's body.

Around 2:30 p.m., several of them helped the swift water rescue team put the rescue boat into the river.

As the afternoon waned on, only eight young men were left, all of them Oldmen except John Welsh, Gabe's pledge mate. They sat on the riverbank overlooking the river, talking, still hoping that Gabe had just gotten lost and wandered off.

The Five Points Volunteer Fire and Rescue Department, headed up by K.D. Giesalhart, kept dragging the river around the sandbar, finding nothing.

One more left at 4:00 p.m. still believing that Gabe had wandered off and would turn up somewhere in Austin.

At 4:46 p.m. they lowered the gaffing hook into the water catching the lower pant leg of Gabe's Levis and pulling his body from the Colorado River 100 yards down river from the sandbar where the Cowboys had been the night before. His body had been caught in some branches to the side, down river from the sandbar.

Gabe's arms were extended, his thumbs tucked into his fists, his lower lip tightly clasped between his teeth. They placed him into the boat on his side. Pink fluid flowed from one side of his nostrils. They pulled the boat onto the land, laying him on his other side. The other nostril exploded with pink fluid, a sure sign of drowning.

AND THEN THERE WERE NONE

The men who dragged the river told us the following Monday that after they had pulled Gabe's body up and laid him on the shore, they looked around for his friends and there were none.

John Welsh told me later that when he realized they had found Gabe's body, he ran as hard and as fast and as far as he could go, fell down on his knees and cried.

COWBOYS MEETINGS

A few hours after Gabe's body was pulled from the river, the Cowboys officers met with lawyers until past midnight.

The next day, all the Cowboys and the Newmen who were present at the initiation met from 9:00 a.m. to 3:00 p.m. at the home of the mother of one of the officers. Four attorneys and a psychologist (a former Cowboy) were present.

There were other weekly meetings after that.

Attorney Randy Leavitt from the Minton law firm in Austin told them he would be representing the Texas Cowboys and that he'd dealt with this stuff before. Mr. Branson, Carl's dad, spoke to them about the "tragedy," then the psychiatrist talked with them. They were told to "expect a lot of media."

~9~

FINAL THOUGHTS FROM TEXAS COWBOYS' STATEMENTS

"Higgins was my pledge brother, my friend and my Texas Cowboy partner. I had known Higgins for two years from the summer before beginning college until now. We went through our pledgeship together and we were close. Higgins was shy, soft-spoken and had a heart of gold. He was generous, funny and an incredible athlete." Newman John Welsh

"Higgins was a Newman. I did not know him well. The first time I met Higgins was at the first meeting of the Cowboys. Higgins and I were not in the same fraternity. I volunteered at Rosedale [The ARC] every Monday at 10:00 a.m. Higgins had a different volunteer time because it was scheduled around the members' class schedules. I am not sure what picnic group Higgins was in. Higgins is one of those quiet guys that you know he's there but you wouldn't notice if he slipped off from the group. I had talked to Higgins a few times during the picnic but not at length and I am not sure what we talked about. I do not remember if Higgins was drinking when [we] talked but everyone was drinking through the night except the brother with the ulcer. Higgins did not strike me as drunk, not at all." Newman Sean Nimmo.

According to Newman Cliff Condrey, written by his lawyer: "Gabe did not appear drunk, his speech wasn't slurred, he never seemed to be having any difficulty, and he never fell or stumbled when they were going down to the river or while they were in that area." Cliff recalled how Gabe had even assisted him once on their way down to the river when

FINAL THOUGHTS FROM TEXAS COWBOYS' STATEMENTS

he himself stumbled. To his knowledge, "Gabe was in good shape and was known to be a good swimmer."

"Until we realized Gabe was gone it was a great time. A unified group of guys." Newman Jacob DeLeon.

"Gabe Higgins had ridden with me to the picnic, and seemed to behave normally, and was in a good mood. I do not think that he would have intentionally hurt himself. Also, Gabe was one of the most likable people that I know, and I can think of no one that would want to harm him." Newman Matt Henehan

Newman Mark Roberton believed that he was "the last one to see Gabe alive."

Newman Jeff Peterson, written by his lawyer: "[Jeff] doesn't think a sober person would go swimming [in] that river with their clothes on. He believes that Gabe's drinking (which Jeff believes was under Gabe's control) and Gabe's own irresponsibility (being told not to go to the river but doing it anyway) may [have been] factors that led to his death."

"It is my feeling that the evening was conducted in a manner that was safe and conscientious." Newman Scott Archer

Oldman Mitchell Fagelman, who was present but not an officer wrote: "On Saturday afternoon, I saw a team lower a boat into the river obviously to search for Gabriel Higgins. At that point, I became ill at the thought that he might have drowned. I did not feel that I could help anymore at that point, and at about 2:00 p.m. I left. I do not believe I have ever met Gabriel Higgins personally, nor do I remember his face from the few Cowboy functions I attended. However, I feel horrible about this tragic accident. I know that this is a terrible experience for everyone involved, especially Gabriel Higgins' family, and I will remember this for the rest of my life."

~10~

THE BANSHEE CRY OF THE DEATH ANGEL

Gabe died sixteen hours before I was notified by Gabe's best friend Brian Thorp, who called me at 5:30 p.m. here in Idaho; 6:30 p.m. Austin time.

Brian did not preface this with: "I have some bad news for you about Gabe." Nor did he say, "Sit down and brace yourself. Something bad has happened."

The fact that it wasn't the police or an official from the university somehow didn't make it official. My ears heard it but my brain didn't accept it. I flipped into denial and stayed there.

I kept saying: "It's OK," after every time he said he was sorry, comforting him! It was like someone else was on the phone with him.

I honestly thought it was a prank call. A couple months earlier, Gabe had his Kappa Sig little brother call me and talk to me as part of his pledging the Kappa Sigs. I don't know why, but I thought this phone call was something along the same category. I was going through the motions and speaking, but my mind and my heart were unable to deal with it.

I didn't hear the name of the city of Bastrop clearly, nor did I write it down or ask him who I could call to confirm it. When he said, "They THINK he drowned," I received it as an uncertainty, and it threw me into even more confusion.

I hadn't slept well the night before. That morning at 6:00 a.m., only a few hours after Gabie died (unbeknownst to me), I bolted up out of bed wide-awake and in sheer panic, got dressed and went for a three-mile walk around the walking path, then over to my folks' house for breakfast. I've never done that before or since.

The day before, in music theory, the teacher told us about the weird banshee type sounds produced by a piano when one of the strings is stroked on the soundboard in the back of the piano. "It sounds like the Banshee cry of the death angel in the movie *Darby O'Gill and the Little People*," he said. So, after class, I rented the video. That night I fell asleep on the couch watching it. It was a haunting movie, very prophetic in retrospect, considering that the reason I was watching it was to hear the death angel sing this eerie, high pitched scream as the death coach came to pick up its victim, Darby O'Gill. I am haunted by the fact that only a couple hours later, it picked up my son.

I felt sick to my stomach and ill at ease all day long, like something terrible was wrong and I couldn't make it right, no matter how hard I tried. I prayed intermittently. I thought at first that it was the fact that I had completely forgotten to take tickets at the choir concert the night before, a work-study job I had. The Music Department secretary filled in for me. I really wasn't sick. It was just a very different, "off" day, unlike any kind of day I'd ever experienced before or since. In my diary, I stated that I felt in a state of panic and dread all day long. I slept a lot and felt like crying for no reason.

At 5:00 p.m., my parents called and asked if I wanted to go to dinner. I said yes. They said they'd pick me up at 5:30. It was exactly 5:30 when Brian Thorp called. Several minutes passed before I got into my car and drove the four blocks to my folks' house.

When I got there, they were sitting in the kitchen waiting for *me* to pick *them* up! Sobbing uncontrollably, hardly able to stand up, I told them that Gabe's friend had called and what he said. I didn't know anything about where the river was, the name of the city (Bastrop), or how to get hold of Brian Thorp. In our confusion and shock, we didn't even think about calling the Kappa Sigma fraternity.

I called the Austin police to try to confirm it. They knew nothing about it. I called the Travis County Police. Nothing. They said they would call us right back. We waited for forty-five minutes to no avail, not knowing what else to do in an effort to confirm it before we started calling relatives.

Still in shock and having no confirmation, I elected *not* to call my other son, Brian. About 6:30 or 7:00 p.m., he called and asked how I was doing. I told him, "Not very well."

He said that he knew about Gabe. He had just called the Kappa Sig house out of the blue to talk to Gabe and they had told him. I was sobbing. I told him that I hadn't called him because I didn't know whether or not it was prank or joke. I wanted to confirm it first.

There were several seconds of silence and he replied, "Mom. You don't need to confirm it. This is no prank."

I know it sounds crazy, but the whole thing didn't sink in until that moment.

Everything else that night was surrealistic, like a foggy nightmare. I didn't want to be there. It was like someone else was going through the movements. I couldn't quit sobbing and crying. My head throbbed and ached.

People kept calling. Relatives. Brian called back later.

I ran back home and found that Brian Thorp had left the number of the Bastrop County Sheriff's office on my answering machine. I called them and a deputy sheriff answered and said that he couldn't give out any information until the body had been properly ID'd, but that they had a nineteen-year old drowning victim from the Colorado River near Bastrop and that his body was in the morgue.

My nephew in California called and gave me the number of the county morgue.

I called the number and asked him if he had a 19-year old drowning victim. He told me yes, he did, but that he couldn't tell me who it was because the body had not been properly identified. He said that if they had found a wallet on him, they could have ID'd him, but there was no wallet. I asked him if he could tell me what he was wearing.

He left the phone and looked, then told me that he had on tan Levi jeans, a white undershirt, a white button down shirt, and cowboy boots. There was no jewelry, no belt, and no wallet.

We were all the more puzzled, because we couldn't imagine how Gabe, who could swim like a fish, could possibly have wound up fully dressed in a river wearing cowboy boots. We asked each other, "How do you swim in cowboy boots?" And I thought to myself, "How could he have been so stupid? That doesn't sound like something Gabe would do."

Tim and Fran, Gabe's dad and step-mom, were out for the evening and didn't find out about Gabe until around 1:00 a.m. Sunday morning, nearly twenty-three hours after Gabe died.

My little sister Dorothy was at work when she was called. She started shaking and went into the bathroom and vomited. Theresa, Gabe's best friend in high school, did the same thing. She was unable to eat for a week and knowing how well Gabe could swim and remembering the pacts they made to each other to be cautious and look out for each other especially when they drank alcohol, she immediately suspected foul play.

I made one last phone call to a pharmacist friend, told her what had happened and asked her how much medicine I could take to guarantee one good night of sleep and make me functional the next day. She told me. I took a sleeping pill, two Aleve's and a Hydrocodone for my pounding headache and went to sleep on Mom and Dad's couch.

I didn't want to go home or be alone.

~11~

I'M O.K. MOM, I'M O.K.

The next morning, Don and I flew to Austin and met with Tim and Fran who had driven over from Galveston. We had dinner together and talked.

They told us that Gabe's body was scheduled to be autopsied the next morning. We found out later that the autopsy, including testing for blood alcohol and drugs, had already been done on Sunday morning before we arrived in Austin. I also found out (years later) that performing an autopsy without parental permission in the accidental death of a person under the age of 21 was within the law.

At dinner, I told all three of them that there were two things I had to do. I had to go to Gabe's room to see where he lived since I'd never been there. I wanted to touch the last things he touched, to smell his clothes, pack up his things and just meditate on him. The other thing I needed to do was to view the river where he died.

I took another sleeping pill combination that night and found myself popping Hydrocodone like it was candy. Whenever my head started aching from crying, I took one, which was all too often.

Monday morning came fast. Tim and Fran had already hired a lawyer from Austin, someone Fran had previously worked with. They rode to Bastrop with him while Don and I took their little red sports car.

The entire ride was a blur. Don began talking about something, and I just disconnected and began thinking about Gabe. I loved him so much. Memories flooded over me. I remembered that little two-year old in diapers who used to steal the football, then his dad running up from behind and swooping him up in his arms and making a touchdown while everyone else just stood there watching. They all cheered. They all loved Gabe.

Then reality would hit and nothing seemed real. Every part of me was numb. My brain was numb. My emotions were frayed and numb. I just sat there in a different world, somewhere I never want to go again.

Do you know what happens when a person's appendix ruptures? The doctor opens up the abdomen, gets out all the infection he can, sterilizes it three times with a saline solution, closes it back up, puts the patient on an IV, and waits for five or six days for the intestines to begin working again. Essentially, the abdomen goes into shock and shuts down.

That's how I felt. Everything seemed to shut down. Life was passing me by and I wasn't connected to it. I dealt with things and talked and cried, but way down, there was a pain so intense that something deep in me was not working. It was like time inside me had stopped and I wasn't able to step into real time. Nor did I want to. I wanted things to stop and go in reverse, kind of like that Superman flick where Lois Lane dies and Superman (Christopher Reeves) flies around the world in a reverse direction with so much super power that the world goes backwards in time. Then he is allowed to deal with the situation again and save her from death.

I just wanted Superman to stop the world and get me off the train or something. Everything was way out of control. I knew I wasn't dreaming. I knew I couldn't stop it. All I could do was to take it a step at a time and allow myself the luxury of crying.

Then the strangest thing happened in the car with Don. I heard this voice, not an audible voice. It was more like a knowing, and it said to me, "Mom, I'm OK. Mom, I'm OK." Over and over. There was a flood of great peace that settled on me for the first time since Gabe died, so I focused on that and let everything else kind of coast by. It helped me deal with it all. I felt Gabe's presence, but I wasn't ready to share this with anybody yet. I felt that no one would understand.

We pulled up to the Bastrop Police Station and a woman met us at the door. She introduced us to everyone and led us into the conference room. I kept trying to be composed, but I was crying so hard that they sat me down and handed me a whole box of Kleenex.

We met with Sheriff Fred Hoskins of Bastrop County who explained that when the police arrived at the ranch on Saturday, no one told them it involved a fraternity and no one mentioned that they were the Texas Cowboys or that this had been an initiation. It was the impression of the police that it was just a group of individuals that were out camping.

Sheriff Hoskins told us that when they got there, the area had been meticulously cleaned. There was no sign that anyone had been camping. There were no campfire embers, there were no bottles or cans lying around, so they had no reason to suspect any drinking. The only thing they found was a couple of beer-can flip-tops. They had no idea how many young men had been there because there were very few vehicles when they arrived. It was his opinion that most of the young men were gone by the time they got there. He said the whole Bastrop police department was surprised when they read the paper and saw the news on TV that it had been a fraternity initiation.

Sheriff Hoskins said there was a strong current on the river and that they had around two accidental deaths due to drowning every year. He said that he'd grown up on the river, as did Lt. David Campos, the investigating officer. Lt. Campos shared with me two years later that he wouldn't have dared swim that river, even during the daytime because of the water moccasins. The only way he would ever have been in or around that river, he said, was in a boat.

Everyone seemed sensitive toward my desire to see the river. They called and made arrangements to view it from the private road across the river from Morgan's property. Deputies Curry and Pence went with us and told us about dragging the river and talking with the boys that day. I took several pictures.

The bank we were on was not as green and full as the Morgan Ranch side. It was full of brown waist high weeds with only one or two trees and had a gentle slope to the river and then dropped off two to four feet straight into the water. The Morgan Ranch side was totally green, full of trees and bushes, with a much higher, steeper bank.

This was NOT a small river. I was a good swimmer and I felt that even in good physical condition, I would question the judgment of anyone desiring to swim across this river. It had tiny ripples on the top, which I detected to be a sign of undercurrents, especially with the large bend in the river. It actually seemed to have two large bends, in a long "S" shape.

The deputies pointed to the sandbar across from us. They explained that the creek access was upstream from the sandbar. It was so far across the river that we could barely see where the creek entered the river. They explained to us that the boys followed the creek down as it led into the river, then onto the upper area of the sandbar.

There was only one sandbar when we saw it on Monday. John Welsh told me three weeks later that there had been two sandbars that night when the boys were on the river. The depth and flow of the river is regulated with small dams or dikes and they had opened them up in the middle of the night due to the rain, which raised the water level and increased the current sometime after 2:00 a.m., Saturday morning.

Deputy Sheriff Pence said a tall young man named Cliff told them that he had walked to the water with Gabe. Cliff told them that Gabe had hesitated getting into the water.

We had so many unanswered questions that we couldn't even come close to trying to guess what happened. Why were they even down on the water? Had they been told to swim across the river as part of the initiation? Why was Gabe fully clothed? Why did he have cowboy boots on?

We had been told that it was an accident. We heard a rumor that the pledges were told to swim to the other side of the river to pick up paddles and to put out a campfire, which sounded like typical and believable fraternity stuff to us. We were also told that some of them had taken their clothes off and were swimming in their shorts. We didn't know what to believe. And in our grief, we couldn't deal very well with sorting it out anyway.

After viewing the river, we had lunch in Austin and then finalized the arrangements for the Memorial service at Weed-Corley-Fish Mortuary, setting it for Wednesday afternoon. Fran and I volunteered to be the ones to "ID" his body. At the last moment, Tim decided to go with us. Don waited in the main room.

The mortician led us to the back of the mortuary. He tried to prepare us for the viewing, and though I knew it was going to be bad, *nothing* could have prepared me for what I saw. He told us that the body had been autopsied and should not be moved because the back of Gabe's head had been taken off during the autopsy (and put back on). He also warned us not to pull the sheet down from his neck because the autopsy procedure had opened his body up and that his body had not been properly prepared yet for burial (we assumed he was not stitched up). He warned us that Gabe was purple in color, as drowning victims are.

We were escorted into a back room where Gabe's nude body laid on a tilted bed of stainless steel, the sheet covering him to his neck. The sight of him took my breath away, and I doubled over sobbing with heaves of pain. I felt as though I had been hit in the stomach and couldn't breathe. My son. My beautiful, gorgeous son. Lifeless. Purple.

The blood drained from my head and every breath I took was labored. Inside I kept screaming, "No, no, no, no. Not Gabe. God, not Gabie. Jesus, God, please not him."

Trembling and crying, I just stood there looking at him. I didn't want to leave him. I didn't want him to be dead. The pit of despair and the pain of sorrow began connecting, and what was numb earlier began to feel. But it was only pain I felt.

It was emotional pain so deep that it was physical pain. I had no control over it. No medicine could take it away. I just throbbed inside. Tears flowed. I bawled and let myself go. I wanted to scream. I was screaming inside.

I touched his skin. It was cold. I knew that he wasn't in that body, but it didn't help much. All I wanted was for Gabe to be alive. Looking at him made me face the fact that he wasn't, which began bringing reality to the surface.

After what seemed an eternity, but was probably only a few minutes, I knew I had to get out of there. I turned and glimpsed at Tim and Fran who were a few steps behind me. What I saw shocked me. Tim was crying as hard as I was. In my pain, I hadn't heard him. Fran was holding him. For a split second I felt envious that he had someone to hold him, someone to lean on. I left the room and met Don in the lobby where we embraced for a long time until I quit sobbing.

Lawyer and Tim at the river
Creek entrance is between them on the other side of the river

Two sandbars where they fought the night before
River level raised over one foot in the early morning
Sandbars were larger the night before

Above: creek entrance is at far right of picture –
2nd Arrow marks top of sandbar night before
Left arrow marks water moccasin nest

Below: Arrow on right marks creek entrance –
2nd Arrow marks top of sandbar night before

Above: Looking up river toward the sandbars
Gabe's body was found on the left in this picture

Below: Looking down river from same vantage point

~12~

THE WAKE

We went back to the hotel in separate cars. Don and I drove together. I told him my head was pounding and I needed a nap. I walked into my room and caught a glance of the room service brochure that pictured the mega chocolate brownie and ice cream dessert with whipped cream on top. My body quickly responded before my brain kicked in, and I found myself on the phone ordering it. Within minutes they delivered TWO of them!

Before I had a chance to sit down and pick the spoon up, Don walked in to ask when we should leave to pick our sister Jeannie up from the airport and also when we were going to the fraternity house that evening. He lifted up the cover on the desserts, grabbed one of the two spoons and began taking monster bites of it while lecturing me on why I shouldn't have ordered such a terribly fattening thing.

I told him it was none of his business on the desert thing. Then I think it kind of turned into a sibling thing. He kept laughing at me and gobbling as much as he could. In between bites, he would keep talking, which I soon realized was to distract me from what he was doing. He mentioned that someone should call the folks and keep them informed, and then concluded that he would. We decided I needed a nap and he would pick our sister Jeannie up. I finally shooed him out of the room, finished eating the whole thing (what was left) and took a nap.

At 7:30 that evening, Don and Jeannie woke me up, gave me some food, and told me to get ready to go, we would be going to Gabe's fraternity house.

By 8:00, Don, Jeannie, Tim, and I were driving to the Kappa Sig house. Fran stayed behind to make phone calls and coordinate relatives coming for the memorial service.

GABE'S ROOM

Tim had called and talked to Harry Painter, the Kappa Sig President, who met us outside the fraternity house and escorted us to Gabie's room. He took us through what struck me as a very late 60's/early 70's dining room with a vaulted ceiling and huge windows along the back. We walked out the sliding glass door onto a small patio, then to a two-story dormer on the left of the main house. Gabe's room was on the second story to the far left end, closest to the street. There were three beautiful white potted lilies outside the door. I stopped briefly to admire them, then took a big breath, asked God for strength, and walked slowly into my son's room, struggling to grasp the reality that he wasn't there anymore.

Not much furniture: bunk beds and some shelves. It looked very lived in. There were five huge garbage bags lined up against one wall toward the back. I was told later they were Gabe's dirty laundry. My immediate attention was given to Jon Faulkner, Gabe's roommate and Brian Thorp, his best friend. Their eyes were red and both boys looked like they'd been through the wringer. They looked like I felt. We just hugged.

They started showing me all his things, including his guitar, pointing out where he sang them to sleep every night before he went to bed. They told me that they loved hearing Gabe sing and play his guitar each night and that they all looked forward to it.

One of Gabe's favorites was "Brown-Eyed Girl." His girlfriend told me later that when he sang it for her he changed it to "Blue-eyed Girl." We stood there talking while Tim looked for clothes for his burial. He found a suit and a nice dress shirt. We found the worn out green T-shirt I had given him a year before on St Patrick's Day that said, "You can tell an Irishman, but you can't tell him much." Gabe was so proud of being Irish we added that to the pile.

Plans of being alone, savoring the last reflection of my son weren't meant to be. Instead, one by one, Gabe's fraternity brothers came into the room and introduced themselves. I could tell they really loved him. They were all dealing with it in their own way. They needed to meet their friend's Mom as much as I needed to meet them.

Tim left to take the clothes to the car and Don was down the hall talking with someone.

THE STUDY ROOM

There were five guys now in Gabe's room and the mood eased when one of them asked, "Do you want to see where Gabe studied?"

"Of course," I said, and was escorted into the next bedroom, which looked like several tornadoes had hit simultaneously. I realized then that the room I just left had probably looked equal to this one before it had been "cleaned" for our visit (thus, the bags).

This study room had a single bed barely visible under the debris, a TV, and two large chairs facing the TV. The more comfortable, overstuffed chair near the back wall was where Gabe had studied the last time on Thursday evening. The milk carton and his beef jerky wrapper were still sitting on the ledge beside the chair he sat in, his homework notes still laying on the floor. I stood there trying to savor every moment and detail, in a hopeless attempt to feel him once more. I was in awe of how quickly one precious life could be taken in what seemed like only moments before.

Several guys were gathered around now and we were laughing about the baseball hat I'd sent Gabe in a care package the semester before. This baseball hat, labeled "Idaho" had hair dangling down the back and when anyone wanted a big laugh, they'd put it on. It could turn a perfectly good-looking guy into somebody nobody knew.

Someone found Gabe's old army helmet and brought it in to show me. They told me that he wore it around the house all the time. It had disgusted one of the guys so much that he swiped it out of Gabe's room and disposed of it by burying it halfway down in one of the large garbage bins that stood outside the back door of the frat house. When Gabe got home from school and discovered it missing, he searched until he found it, washed it off, put it back on his head and had worn it every day since then.

There were so many guys gathered by now in this small room, there really wasn't any place to sit down. Brian suggested moving to the chapter room.

THE CHAPTER ROOM

Brian and Jon walked with me down through the dining room area to the Chapter Room on the other side of the fraternity house. It was a large, beautiful room with four lovely new couches. The walls were covered with pictures of the previous years of Kappa Sigma fraternity brothers, various awards, and a couple of elk heads that must have been someone's trophies. My first impression was that it was a pretty great room, except the elk heads made me wonder if some alumnus' wife refused to allow them in her home and by elimination they just found a good home here.

It was such a big room with only the three of us. I was told the others were calling the rest of the guys to come.

I looked around at the pictures, then sat down and said, "So tell me some stories about Gabe."

The stories rolled.

TEXAS A&M KAPPA SIGS

Brian Thorp smiled and began reminiscing about the first few weeks of Gabe's freshman year when they both visited the Kappa Sig fraternity house at Texas A&M in College Station, UT's rival school. It was a much smaller fraternity. As he began, I remembered hearing this story before from Gabe, but I relished hearing it again.

The Texas A&M Kappa Sigs were very cordial to Brian and Gabe, staying up late watching movies with them. When the last movie ended early in the morning, each of the fraternity guys excused themselves, said goodnight and went to bed, leaving Gabe and Brian to sleep on their couches.

The walls of their Chapter Room were lined with really great fraternity paddles and the temptation overtook the two. They both grabbed the two biggest, most decorated paddles and left.

The next morning in Austin, they showed everyone their trophy paddles with big smiles. Simultaneously, the president of the Texas A&M Kappa Sigs was talking to the president of the UT Kappa Sigs and told him that the paddles had better be back on their walls the next weekend, "or else."

Late the next Saturday night, Brian and Gabe reluctantly drove over to College Station and in the silence of the wee hours, they left the trophy paddles leaned up against the front door of the Kappa Sig house, tip toeing away in the silence of the night. Brian later produced pictures someone took of the two of them (there must have been a third person with them) in front of the Texas A & M Kappa Sig bus, peeing on the paddles before they gave them back. (I'm not proud of what they did, but I have to be honest and tell the whole story.)

PADRE ISLAND TRIP

Greg Booth, another close friend of Gabe's, was next. They were Kappa Sig pledge mates and had also been "suite mates," sharing a bathroom at the Kappa Sig house. A few weeks into school their sophomore year, they went on a road trip to Padre Island fishing.

Before Gabe was born, his dad, Brian and I spent many weekends driving the full length of the island, camping out and fishing since it was only an hour's drive away from where we lived.

When Greg and Gabe got there, they walked into a fishing store and asked to rent some fishing poles. The guy asked, "What are you fishing for?"

They looked at each other and drew a blank. Gabe, the mighty fisherman quickly replied, "Shark!"

I can see the salesman turning his head to laugh. He charged them $3.00 each for the poles and since they thought: "bigger was better," they picked out the largest fishing poles they could find. They caught one small fish, slept on the beach and thought they were kings.

RUSHIN'

Chad Shimoitis, one of Gabe's pledge brothers, shared that when they were both pledging Kappa Sigs, Gabe was out in front of the fraternity house washing someone's car. Chad walked up from behind him and asked, "Are you rushin'?"

Gabe answered, "No. I'm from Idaho."

No matter how much grief any of us had been in, everyone laughed at that one. I looked around to see that the whole room had filled up with about fifty guys, twelve girls, some parents, Tim, Don, Jeannie, and I. I took a few pictures and handed my camera to one of the guys to take more.

THE EARRING
Andrew Sorrell, one of the older Kappa Sigs spoke. He said that when Gabe began pledging, he had an earring in his left ear. Andrew wasn't at all impressed with it and told Gabe that the earring was NOT going to work out.

Gabe simply responded with, "OK," took the earring out and put it in his pocket. Andrew said that the gesture touched his heart and he knew Gabe would be "in" with no problem.

Someone else added to that, and said that he had told Gabe earlier that there was a group of Kappa Sigs that "to impress them was no big thing," and then there was another group that he really needed to impress: like, wear the right kind of clothes, say the right things. Andrew was one of the latter. Everyone laughed and someone else added that Gabe had on shorts and tennis shoes that night.

I told them that his earring was left over from high school. A month before graduation, Gabe and I drove to Idaho Falls for his last doctor checkup after his knee surgery and since he was given a clean bill of health, he caught me at a weak moment later in the mall. I actually gave him my permission to get the earring with the stipulation that he would only wear it through the summer.

DOING LAUNDRY
During Gabe's first year at UT, he lived in the Dobie Center, a high rise for freshmen a block off campus. The first time he had to launder his clothes (he hated doing his laundry), he looked in the phone book and found a Laundromat close, bundled up his things, borrowed a car, loaded it up, and headed out only to find that the Laundromat was directly across the street. He could have walked over!

SHOPPING AT THE MALL
One weekend that winter when Crystal was visiting from Dallas, Gabe's roommate Jon joined Gabe and Crystal on a trip to the shopping mall. Gabe found a very plain brown-striped sweater he fell in love with. Holding it up to his face, he asked, "What d'ya think?"

Pause, no answer.

"I could wear this fourteen days without having to wash it! Perfect, huh?"

Jon and Crystal looked at each other, like: "Is this guy for real?" Then belly laughed. They had no other choice but to agree with him. He purchased it. And wore it often, I heard.

They decided to get something to eat at one of the many lunch places. Gabe said, "We have to have corn dogs."

They replied, "Why do we have to have corn dogs?"

He answered, "When you go to the mall, you always get corn dogs!"

They laughed and obligingly ate corn dogs with him.

I explained that during the summer Gabe turned seven years old, we both loved corn dogs so much that the two of us made several trips to the mall each week for them. It was probably why trips to the mall became synonymous with corn dogs for Gabe.

RIDING THE BUS

Tim was next. He shared that Gabe was always a shy child growing up. When Gabe moved to Galveston to live with them in his junior year of high school, they immediately signed him up for football. This meant practices every night after school. They told him he would have to take the bus home to the island since they both worked and didn't get home until around 5:30 or 6:00 p.m.

Gabe got home every night around 7:00 p.m. They thought nothing of it until two weeks later when he started getting home around 6:00 p.m. They asked him why and he said that he had been taking the bus the long way around Galveston Island to get home. It took him two weeks to realize that he was on the wrong bus! The bus pick-up across the street went the other direction and was much shorter.

He had been too shy to ask anyone.

MOVING

One of the girls shared that when she was moving into a different apartment, Gabe just showed up unexpectedly, bright and cheery, and helped her unpack her car and move in. They had been good friends ever since.

THE SENIOR PROM

Tommy Carter was one of Gabe's best friends their freshman year. They lived next door to each other in the Dobie Center and had both pledged Kappa Sigs. He introduced his folks, sister, and girlfriend, all sitting next to him. They all came down from Dallas to be with Tommy after hearing about Gabe. His folks shared that they really liked Gabe and that he had come to Dallas with their son a few times to spend the weekend.

Tommy told us that in the spring of their freshman year, it was his little sister's Senior Prom and since he was dating his sister's best friend, they all decided to rent a limousine and make it a four couple date with two more of his little sister's girlfriends.

Tommy was given the job of finding three other fraternity guys for dates: one for his sister and two others for her two friends. He found two guys for the two friends, but he was having a hard time finding a suitable young gentleman to escort his sister. He confided in Gabe one day, "I need to find a guy who's young enough for my sister and a really nice guy."

Gabe immediately replied, "I'm young enough and I'm a really nice guy!"

Tommy laughed and looked no further. Gabe's honesty and transparency was refreshing. After the prom, he queried Gabe: "You didn't do anything with my little sister, did you?"

Gabe replied, "I'll never tell," which drove Tommy nuts.

His mom immediately clarified that Gabe was a perfect gentleman through the whole weekend, and they thought very highly of him.

PLAYING BASKETBALL

Every night before and after dinner, even though he had to wear a brace on his leg from the knee operation, Gabe played basketball on the court in the backyard of the Kappa Sig house.

A guy nicknamed Onion told us that at the beginning of the spring semester that year, they chose two-man teams for the fraternity basketball games. No one chose Onion. As he spoke, I noticed that it was probably because he was a little on the short side.

Gabe, at 5'9", told Onion that he would duo with him. But he made the rules clear: "Don't try to make any baskets. Just get the ball and throw it to me."

Onion did as he was told and they were undefeated.

CRYSTAL

There were other stories. The room was now filled with a lovely warm feeling instead of the death grip that grief had engulfed us in earlier. We were laughing and missing this person we all had grown to love and regard.

We stayed to talk with many of the young men and women who introduced themselves to Don, Tim, Jeannie, and me, expressing their condolences. It impressed me that they were such nice looking, polite, and intelligent young people, and also that his death had touched all of them in such a deep and profound way. It was a healing time for all of us.

This was when I met Crystal, Gabe's girlfriend. I recognized her from the pictures Gabe had shown me at Christmas. She was very beautiful with long gorgeous blonde hair. In her pictures, she looked vibrant, but that night she looked very pale and shaken up. In fact, her hands were shaking a little as she introduced herself. We hugged and talked and cried. I gave her my pinky ring that Gabe had given me when he was in high school.

She told me later that she didn't know whether or not she should even talk to me, in fear that I might not receive her. They told her earlier at the fraternity house not to go into Gabe's room where I was and to respect my space. So the fact that I received and regarded her, affirmed her. I shared with her what Gabe had told me at Christmas, that he really cared for her.

THE NEWMEN'S TEARS

I excused myself, and on my way to the ladies room, there were a couple of Texas Cowboy pledges from another fraternity sitting on the steps outside the Chapter Room. They were very shaken up. One was crying and in pretty bad shape. They stopped me and asked if I was Gabe's Mom. They told me that they were very sorry about Gabe's death. I sat down on the steps beside the one who was having the hardest time, put my arm around him, and consoled him that it had just been an accident and that they didn't need to beat themselves up about it.

In their grief they seemed to project a depth of guilt I had not picked up from any of Gabe's Kappa Sig friends. It took me by surprise as I was convinced at that time that it had been totally an accident. It was the first time I felt a glimmer of the possibility of other circumstances.

We said our goodbyes around midnight and left. At the hotel I took the pill combo and fell asleep.

Two story dormer north of Kappa Sig house
Gabe's room was top, left corner

Roommate Jon and Best friend Brian
The bottom bunk is Gabe's
Kappa Sig enters front door of room

THE WAKE

Study room with friends after pre-final's tornado hit
Gabe studied in dark blue chair night before
Milk carton and beef jerky wrapper on counter
Homework notes on floor

The Wake
Telling "Gabe" stories

THE WAKE

Back of Kappa Sig house with pool
Ruth with Kappa Sig guys

Basketball Court and Pool

With best friend, Brian

Kappa Sig house at Texas A & M
Returning the paddles

Friend Greg at Padre Island fishing pier. Monster pole, monster fish
Gabe in brown-stripped sweater

Kappa Sig Pledge Class – Gabe is in the dark blue shirt, middle right
Kappa Sig Christmas Party – below. Gabe is middle, far left in lone star hat

Gabe pretending to be a Cowboy with Chewing tobacco in his mouth (his tongue)

Hawaiian Party

KAPPA SIGMA
"Round-up"
April 7, 1995

Uncle Donnie and the helmet with Gabe's friends Jon and Greg

Helmet encased in entryway at Kappa Sig house

THE WAKE

After the Memorial Service at friends' apartment
Carter and little brother Chris play Gabe's songs

~13~

"WISH YOU WERE HERE"
The Memorial Service

I woke up crying. At breakfast, we talked about how the grief seemed to come in waves. Just one thought or mention of Gabe and grief would roll over us like an ocean wave. At the time I selfishly thought I was the only one experiencing deep grief, since I was the mother. It was amazing to me to see that so many others were going through the same thing.

Gabe's picture was on the front page of both the *Austin American-Statesman* and the *Daily Texan*. His story was the first one mentioned on the evening news. We remarked to each other that they knew more than we did, and even at that, it wasn't much.

Tuesday, after lunch, we all drove to the funeral home to meet with the minister and finalize the memorial service. It was a whirlwind that seemed more like a hurricane.

The viewing was supposed to have begun at 7:00 p.m., Tuesday evening. I spent the first 45 minutes in the bathroom feeling sick with an upset stomach, probably from taking so much Hydrocodone. Most of that night was a blur. We had been asked earlier for permission from the Texas Cowboys to come to the viewing wearing their "gear" Cowboy uniforms (white shirts, wheat levis, boots, chaps, and hats). While we really didn't mind it, we hadn't responded quickly enough for them to do it. They all showed up in suits and ties.

A long line of people curved back around the corner and out of sight. Tim and I stood a few feet away from the casket and about halfway through it all, I became overwhelmed with grief that this line I was standing in could have and should have been a receiving line of a happier occasion, like Gabe's wedding or something, not a line eight steps away from his dead body.

Gorgeous girls kept coming up to me, hugging me and telling me how much they liked Gabe. Typically they said: "I knew Gabe and thought he was one of the nicest, sweetest guys I've ever known. I just loved him. He was so much fun to be with." Some dated him, some hadn't.

At the same time this was going on, I reflected about Gabe asking me his senior year after his girlfriend had just dumped him, "Mom, do you think I'll ever have any girlfriends?" I assured him that he would. He was too good-looking, friendly, talented and smart not to. Besides, I told him, girls liked guys like him who were fun to be with, kind and considerate. Still, he wondered. I stood there at the viewing pondering if Gabe was aware of all this.

Back at the hotel the next morning, all of the family and extended family met in one room down the hall and ate breakfast together. Don found Gabe's old army helmet, which he wore all morning. Tim's older brother Mike and my older brother Don had both been Air Force pilots in Viet Nam. Since they both married two sisters, it made for interesting conversation: all six of our kids were double cousins.

When we arrived that afternoon, the funeral home was packed. Don, Jeannie and I were escorted to a small room behind the sanctuary where Tim, Fran, Mike and their mother (Gabe's grandmother), were waiting. We were all ushered into the large room packed with people and seated in the front row, in front of the casket.

It was all I could do to focus on just making it through the service by looking at the little brown stuffed dog that sat on top of the casket holding a heart that said, "I love you." It had been on Gabe's bed earlier and it brought me to reflect on his gentle, sweet heart and precious spirit. Someone handed me a box of Kleenex.

I sat through both the memorial service in Austin and the funeral service three days later in Pocatello, yelling at God (inside myself): *"Why did Gabe die, Lord? Why did you let him die? If you're such a great God, why didn't you save him? Why didn't your angels escort Gabe to the top of the water?"* It was years later that I finally accepted that Gabe *was* in a safe place and that the angels actually *did* escort him to the top of the water … and into heaven.

The room was packed. People were standing in the back and many stood outside. "The angels weep for what might have been," the Reverend Craig Sommer said. "What matters is that the young man was loved, incredibly so."

Seven of Gabe's closest friends spoke at the funeral: three guys and four girls.

"To me, Gabe was one of the best," Jon Faulkner began, adding that he and Gabe were the only ones in the Kappa Sig fraternity who were not born and raised in Texas. With an exception of Gabe's junior year, neither of them went to high school in Texas. Jon explained that anytime anyone started talking about their high school years, like at a party, he and Gabe would make up their own flamboyant stories about a fictitious high school they went to somewhere in Texas.

Gabe had earned Jon's respect and admiration because "He stood up for me on numerous occasions and came to my defense when I needed a friend. I never really thanked him for that. He always stood up for what he believed in."

I had already asked Chris Kline, Gabe's little brother in the Kappa Sigs and Carter Shackleford (who later became president of the Kappa Sigs) if they would play a couple of Gabe's favorite songs at the memorial service. They were excited to do it. Gabe had been teaching Chris how to play the guitar that semester. I looked forward to that performance as the highlight of the whole memorial service. But the minister forgot to call them up. When the service was over, I immediately ran up to the minister and asked him to call the two up to the front to play. He said it was too late, and we were quickly escorted to a back room as everyone was waiting for the family to leave before they could exit.

We were in the back room only a moment when I heard a faint guitar and someone singing. I rushed back into the main room to see Carter and Chris seated in the front, their friends gathered around them listening, as they sang two of Gabe's favorites: "Knockin' On Heaven's Door," and "Wish You Were Here," by Pink Floyd. It was so good.

There was a hush over the half empty room. Everyone turned to listen. All movement stopped and for a few brief moments, it was as if I could hear Gabe's heart singing to me. It was like being in some kind of dreamy state when two things are happening at once and you hear music from far away. My spirit soared with delight as I closed my eyes and listened. When they finished, the room exploded with applause, many of us in tears. It was one of those moments you wish you could capture and fasten to a magnet and put on the fridge to remember forever! It was by far the best part of the whole day!

Don grabbed the little brown dog that said "I Love You" and handed it to me. Jeannie and I grabbed some flowers and the three of us left through the back door. We stuffed Jeannie in the small space behind the bucket seats of Tim's little red sports car and the three of us left for the Kappa Sig house.

They served dinner a little early. It looked really good, but I couldn't eat. There were people everywhere: lots of hugs and warm conversations even though we were all in a state of shock and grief. A short time later, a sweet fragrance filled the room, and I turned to see one whole side of the dining room filled with huge bouquets of flowers, three tiers of bleachers deep. Most of the flowers were from other fraternities and sororities who knew and loved Gabe.

The fraternity guys were exceptionally gracious and kind to us. Carter Shackleford, Brian Thorp, and Jon Faulkner escorted me around the perimeter of the back yard, showing me the six-foot wooden fence along the back that Gabe and Carter had painted the summer before when they were the only two staying in the fraternity house. I laughed at Carter when he told me that the two of them had painted the fence. I told him I knew the truth: Carter did most of the painting while Gabe watched. He laughed and agreed, surprised that I knew my son that well. Gabe *never* liked to paint; it was like punishment to him!

We talked about Gabe. Jon told me that he was really laid back, always in a good mood and easy to live with. The others agreed. Many times whenever they had problems, like with girls, they would go talk with Gabe and get his perspective on the situation. He seemed to have a knack for counseling and reassuring them.

They showed me the basketball court where Gabe played every night, and the greenish tinted pool, which looked like something that could have easily doubled for the "Black Lagoon." They told me all about their parties and the contraptions they built, like the Hawaiian party the month before. They had filled the dining room with six inches of sand, opened the sliding glass doors to the backyard patio and built a seven-foot platform in the middle of the patio with a slide into the pool. I noticed there was no grass growing near the house, just a lot of sand. They laughed and admitted that it was left over from the party.

We were invited over to the girls' apartment two blocks away by a couple of Gabe's closest *girl* friends. Once there, we encouraged Carter and Chris to sing a repeat performance of the two songs they had sung at the end of the funeral. There wasn't a dry eye in the room. It touched me that his friends wanted Don, Jeannie and I to be a part of this. It blessed me to have experienced the love and deep regard Gabe's closest friends had for him.

It was dark when we left their apartment. As Crystal and I slowly walked behind Don and Jeannie back to the fraternity house, I bared my heart to her and told her that I had felt Gabie's sweet voice speaking to me earlier, "I'm OK, Mom," over and over and that it had greatly comforted me. Her eyes got big and she told me that Gabe had spoken to her too and was saying much the same thing, "Baby, I'm OK and everything'll be all right," over and over just the same way he had been speaking to me.

~14~

WHAT REALLY HAPPENED TO COWBOYS

Testimonies from former Texas Cowboys

AFTER THE MEMORIAL SERVICE

Rumors were flying. None of us could figure out what happened. Our first encounter with anyone who seemed to know anything was at the Kappa Sig fraternity after the memorial service.

After everyone had eaten, we each grabbed a pop and stood outside the sliding glass door on the patio in the shade talking. In those conversations, I was told that the Kappa Sigs had parties that involved drinking almost every weekend. Also that Gabe was not a reckless type of person. He didn't get drunk and do crazy things. That was probably one of the reasons why many of us had problems accepting his death as one due to his carelessness like some people claimed. It didn't make much sense.

One of those conversations I had was with four or five guys and went something like this.

Me: "So, come on, be honest, what do you guys know and what do you really think happened on the river? I have a problem trying to figure out how in the world Gabe could have drowned fully clothed with cowboy boots on."

Kappa Sig: "I heard they were told to swim the river to pick up axe handles on the other side and swim back with them."

Another Kappa Sig: "I heard the same thing, that it was part of the initiation, and that they had to put out a fire on the other side."

Me: "Oh yeah? And how would they do that?"

Eyes caught each other, then smiles: "Probably urinating on it! Ha! Ha! Ha! Ha! Ha!"

Me: "O.K. But what I don't understand is why Gabe would have gone swimming, drunk, in a river he wasn't familiar with in the first place. I mean, he was a good swimmer and was smarter than that! I thought I taught him better than that."

Kappa Sig: "Yeah, well guys do crazy, stupid things when they're drinking."

Another Kappa Sig: "It was their initiation. Things happen."

Me: "What are you guys talking about?" I hesitated, "You mean hazing?"

A quiet fell over the group. They lowered their heads. One guy spoke slowly, "Well, Yeah. ALL the Greeks do it. It's tradition. We do it a little in the Kappa Sigs. But nothing like the Cowboys."

Then the guy standing directly to my right, John Hemphling, looked me straight in the eye and said something like this: "Mrs. Higgins, if I had any inkling that they were going to haze Gabe or hurt him in any way, I would have been there in a heartbeat. I would have defended Gabe if it took everything I had and I would have gotten him out of there."

John was a stately, tall, well-spoken young man, the ex-president of the Kappa Sigma fraternity and a former Texas Cowboy who graduated a year or two earlier. What he said was good enough for me, so I put the thought of the Cowboys hazing Gabe completely out of my mind.

Two and a half weeks later, when I was back in Austin to hire my lawyer, I stayed with the Hemphlings, a very gracious family. At that point, even after discussing the possibility of hazing with my lawyer, I truly believed that it was just "an unfortunate accident" like the Cowboys claimed it was. It really didn't sink in until a few weeks after that, that there truly might have been hazing involved, with activities that had endangered Gabe's life.

TRADITION

Hazing has always been a serious part of tradition in the Texas Cowboys. The pledges knew to expect some of it, and were willing to endure whatever was asked of them to earn the privilege of belonging to this honorable group. The Cowboys held two initiations a year. Years before, they changed the name of the initiations to "picnic," inferring that they quit hazing. Minor things varied, but the main program stayed the same. "To be a Texas Cowboy, you had to go through the tap-in, the pledge process, and the picnic at the end." (Jim Hawley interview)

And they all involved hazing.

THE INTERVIEWS
TAP-IN
In 1963 when Jim Hawley pledged, it didn't involve drinking, and the *tap-in* didn't involve paddling. He was picked up late at night, taken 20 miles out of town and dumped in a field at 3:00 in the morning. It was called the "Traditional Walk."[1]

THE PROCESS
After the applications into the Texas Cowboys were turned into the Dean of Students Office and the interviews completed, the prospective Newmen would wait to see if they were accepted. The Dean of Students office decided who was accepted, then called each of the fraternities. Older fraternity brothers who were Texas Cowboys would notify the initiates. Independent Texas Cowboys notified independent pledges. The scenario usually involved being picked up and taken to a tavern off Lamar Street in Austin where the pledges and Cowboys would drink and visit.

You'd think that most of the Newmen pledges would have known they were going to be paddled for *tap-in* because somebody in their fraternities would have told them. In Gabe's case, his older brothers in the fraternity did inform him. My guess is that some of the Newmen didn't have a clue about what to expect. In Lance Watson's case in the spring of 1982, he didn't know because he was an independent and had no older "brother" to inform him.

LANCE WATSON
After Watson was picked up, he was told: "You go through this process if you're going to become a Texas Cowboy. They've always done it this way; they'll do it this way this semester and in the future." Also: "This is part of the tradition; this is a part of the past, and what we're going to do tonight to be a Cowboy is called *tap-in*."

At Lance's *tap-in*, the fifteen pledges were blindfolded and taken to a secluded, abandoned apartment where they waited downstairs. They were taken two at a time to an upstairs room where there were three or four Cowboys in the room with two-fisted paddles about the size of baseball bats that were held about the same way.

A 1987 report from the Presidential Commission on Fraternal Organizations at the University of Texas reported: "The two-handed paddles allowed more force to be applied with considerably greater effect." It added, "Perhaps the result is found to be that one Cowboy swinging a two-handed paddle could lift an initiate off his feet." [2]

He was called to the upstairs room where they grabbed his hands and asked him to bend over and put his hands either on the back of the couch or in their hands. They said to him, "You can do it, man," "You're the best," "Hang in there," and "Come on, Lance; you're going to be a Cowboy."

Then, one at a time, they hit him with everything they had. The last guy to have the paddle would hand it to the next guy who would step back and swing into him. Each Cowboy took three swings at him. "They would just come into me as hard as they could, one at a time." After three paddles, Lance was sent downstairs to wait his turn again. The fifteen Cowboys giving the paddlings rotated so all of them would get three swings at each initiate.

"Everybody wanted to be a Cowboy," Lance, who is now a Southern Baptist Minister, said in his deposition. "I mean, the Texas Cowboys are a traditional group, and most of the guys would give an arm or a leg to be in the group. So I was excited about it and I had a lot of pride and said, 'Well, if everybody is doing it, I'm going to do it,' and I was just swept up into everything that was going on."

He said he didn't remember anything else that went on that night, "except drinking beforehand, drinking during, and ... I just remember the last guy that hit me. His first swings were like everybody else's third swings. I mean he would hit with everything he had. And after being hit two times by this guy, they grabbed me and it just broke me. I mean I was broken. I was down on my knees and they were holding me and saying, 'Come on, hang in there.' And I said, 'That's it.' I knew that I had taken all I could take and they kept encouraging me, kept rooting me on, saying: 'Oh, you can take the last one' and 'you can do it, everybody does it.'

"I turned around and I looked at him and I said, 'If you're going to hit me, hit me,' and I yelled at him with everything I had and, of course, he did. And he almost – and he almost – you know, they ruptured a guy's spleen the year before."

In Watson's *tap-in*, each candidate received forty-five paddlings. An hour and a half later, most of them anesthetized and drunk, they were just glad it was all over. [3]

JAKE FISHER

Tap-in was a little different for 19-year old Newman/pledge Jake Fisher who pledged the Texas Cowboys a few years before Gabe died.

Jake said that a couple of days after his interview with the UT officials, he received a phone call to be in his room at a certain time. Four or five Cowboys in full Cowboy regalia picked him up and told him he would not be home that night.

"Before joining the Cowboys, I was concerned about hazing, but I thought that since the University was involved with the organization to the great extent it was, that hazing, if there was any, would not be bad."

They took Jake to a restaurant where there were other Cowboys drinking. He explained that he didn't drink, which roused a snicker from one of the Cowboys. After fifteen minutes, two guys came up to him and told him to go with them. They took him outside.

"After that, everything changed. The Oldmen were screaming at us and pushing us around. They pushed me into a truck and as soon as I was in, a Cowboy handed me a drink and told me to drink it." Jake told him he wasn't a drinker, but the Cowboy responded, "Shut up and drink it."

"They were making us drink enormous amounts of malt liquor. They would say things like, 'Before we get to the traffic light, you have to have finished drinking this.'"

That night was independents *tap-in* night and there were 12 prospective independent Newmen/ pledges. In Jake's group, three Cowboys were in charge.

"We drove around for awhile and they took us over to the Ex-Students Association Building in front of the Bevo statue and they were making us recite things about the history of the Cowboys. We were being forced to drink the whole time. We had to address the Oldmen as 'Mother Fucker' whenever we spoke to one of them.

"We were taken to the garage of a house one of the Cowboys lived in.

Two other trucks with pledges and Oldmen joined us there at the garage. There was a gravel floor in the garage and the Oldmen were kicking gravel on us and screaming at us and pushing the Newmen around. By this time everyone was really drunk. Some of the Oldmen were getting in fights. They would bring in bags of malt liquor and tell us to drink all of it in the next 30 minutes or they would beat us."

"We were told to go into the garage. They circled around us holding the paddles. They told us that if anyone grabbed the paddle they would knock the crap out of them. One of the guys did grab the paddle by mistake and they hit him four times.

"We had to read the Cowboys' creed and they put their chaps on us. By this time everyone was too drunk to read. Then the *tap-in* was over and they took us back."

The next afternoon, the pledges were taken to a ranch. They rode in trucks: two Newmen in the back and one in front in the cab with two Oldmen. "The whole time they forced us to drink."

The two Oldmen would scream at the guy in the cab of the truck. They stopped every ten minutes to switch Newmen.

After they got there they were made to walk like ducks in a line with their hands on the shoulder of the guy ahead of them. "If our hands fell off, they would scream at us. They made us do this for a long time."

One of them had someone read a passage about Cowboys, even though he was so drunk he could hardly read. The point of the piece he read was that they had the potential of being Cowboys, but there were a lot of physical tests yet that they had to face. They were told that if they thought they could handle it, to stand up. They all stood up and took their blindfolds off.

The Oldmen left all of them there. They had to walk four to six miles to a Circle K and call a friend to come and get them. (This was before cell phones)

Two days later, Jake got a call and was told to meet at the same garage they did before. After all the pledges arrived, the Cowboys surrounded them with paddles in their hands. They laid out the rules. The pledges were told they could not be seen on or off campus either by a Cowboy or friend of a Cowboy. If they were, they would be paddled. They were told if they were seen on campus, it would not be as bad as if they were seen off campus. If they were seen down on Sixth Street or at a party, they would come down hard on them.

The week after the *tap-in*, they were at a ranch and were forced to drink. Everyone was really drunk. He said they read a thing on being a Cowboy and it was all about facing physical danger with strength and without fear.

Later, "They told us each what amount of money we were expected to raise each week," Jake related. "I was told I had to raise $1000 a week. Some guys were told $700 or $800. I don't know how they arrived at the amount for each Newman. We were told that if we didn't raise the money we would be hazed.

"The major forms of hazing they did were paddling and cattle prodding. The less you raised, the worse the hazing would be. I would have to sell 10 full-page ads a week for the music festival program to raise $1000. Most pledges just cut checks themselves to the Cowboys.

"We were sworn to secrecy at this meeting. We were told that we could not tell our friends what went on. We were told that we should have pride and bravery in the face of danger. They said that if anyone talked, there would be hell to pay."

He added, "If you didn't raise the money, they beat you more." And, "No one was able to raise their money."

One night after one of the meetings, Jake was approached by one of the Cowboys, who told him that he had personally lost a lot of self-respect the semester he went through pledging and that he felt Jake was just like him. The Cowboy encouraged him to consider not going through it.

Jake conferred with another Cowboy, "a really nice guy," who told him that when he was getting hazed, he would sit up in his room crying some nights. Though it was unheard of for a Cowboy to drop out, Jake decided he would.

On March 2nd, Texas Independence Day, Jake was not in uniform and the dean of students told him to come to her office. She set up an appointment for him to meet with Dr. James Vick, the head Dean of Students. The night before that meeting, someone threw a rock through Jake's window.

When Jake met with Dr. Vick, he told him everything that had happened. "Dr. Vick did not look surprised. He told me that he had heard all of this before.

"I then realized that the whole time I was being interviewed for the Cowboys, the UT officials sat there and knew I was going to be hazed.

This realization made me angry. I asked him why he hadn't done anything if he knew all of this.

"He said that they needed a student who was willing to speak out. I asked him why he didn't have the Cowboys followed or video taped ... if they had been doing something else illegal like gambling or prostitution, it would be handled that way."

After Jake got out of the Cowboys, he continued to hear stories about what went on. He heard that the Cowboys made the pledges line up facing a wall. Then they were touched on the back of the legs with a cattle prod so that their knees would hit the wall. He also heard that they made pledges hold onto the cattle prod as long as they could to test their strength.

One of his friends, a Cowboy pledge, was pulled out of his bed on "OU Weekend" [University of Texas vs. Oklahoma University football game], and paddled in front of a room full of girls and Cowboys, "just to see what he was made of."

Newmen pledges continued to tell him about the weekly hazing that occurred, dependent on the money each pledge turned in. No one made the amount of money they were required to make, so everyone got hazed.

They were told to always wear jeans and never wear shorts to any function because they would be paddled. They used to talk about what kind of jeans were the best to wear, Wranglers or Levis when they got hit.

His friend showed him the bruises on his butt and legs from where he was paddled from his "picnic."

"He told me that 'picnic' was the worst night of hazing. My friend told me he was hit 30 times and was hospitalized. Three different people told me on three different occasions that at the picnic they hit you 'until you bleed to your boots.' They also told me that someone got urinated on, and that the Newmen had to eat Copenhagen between two slices of bread." [4]

LANCE WATSON INTERVIEW

Lance Watson said he believed that the initiation-picnic was the longest night of his life. "The picnic at the end of the semester was the final part of the pledgeship process. It was the last part of being a Cowboy, and if you made it through the *tap-in* and you made it through earning the money, all you had to do was get through the picnic and you'd be a Texas Cowboy." [5]

THE INITIATION-PICNIC

Watson, who had been a UT Cheerleader and had played on the basketball team, was selected to be a Cowboy the spring of 1982. One night a group of Cowboys picked him up along with the ATO (Alpha Tau Omega) fraternity, even though he was an independent. The Cowboys blindfolded all of the pledges and put them in the back seat. They were told, "We're going to spend the evening somewhere and the next day you'll be a Cowboy."

In the car on the way to the ranch they were told they were going to play "Name That Tune." The Cowboys told them to put their hands on the back of the front seat. On the top of the seat, unseen by them, laid a cattle prod. The Cowboys turned the radio to a station they wanted and then gave the Newmen three seconds to name the tune. "When they didn't, they'd 'zzzz,' zap them with a cattle prod, 'shocking the fool out of our hands.'" The pledges tried making up names to the songs to no avail. This went on for the entire 45-minute drive.

That night at the picnic, they played, "Let's Make a Deal." They had a choice of three doors. If they chose the first door, they would have to take shots of tequila. Behind the second door was the two-fisted paddle, from which they received two or three "licks" from the paddles. Behind door number three was the cattle prod. "There wasn't any arguing. There were no other choices. All of the Newmen obliged because 'Everybody wanted to be a Cowboy.'"

"There was lots of drinking. Because of the peer pressure, if you didn't drink as much, you were looked upon as a wuss. You were looked upon as, 'You can't handle it.' If you couldn't handle the beating and the paddling, you know, you were looked upon as, 'You're not a real man,' or 'You can't handle the close-knitness of the group.'"

"I was naïve," he said. "I didn't know what was coming and thus, I didn't have to think about it." [6]

SCOTT SCARBOROUGH
THE INITIATION-PICNIC

After Lance Watson became a Cowboy, he talked his friend Scott Scarborough into joining the Cowboys because Scott was Students'

Association President in 1983, and they both felt that after Scott became a Cowboy, the Cowboys would listen to him and quit hazing.

Similar to Lance's experience, one Friday afternoon Scott was picked up by some Cowboys who were fully clothed in their uniforms. They told him to pack enough clothes to be gone overnight. He rode in a truck with two or three other Newmen and some Cowboys out to a ranch.

While en route, the Newmen were made to drink a lot of beer and grab hold of a fully charged cattle prod. The Cowboys encouraged the Newmen to drink as much alcohol as possible. Scott arrived at the ranch, and they played poker around a campfire and received "swats" or were shocked with cattle prods if they lost.

He felt the reason why they were drinking so heavily was to numb their bodies so that they would not feel as much pain the following morning.

It was during the events of the following morning after the "hell night" initiation, that Scott Scarborough realized "this wasn't going to be a picnic." [7]

In Lance Watson's deposition, he tells graphically what happened during his initiation:

In the early morning after the evening of the picnic [it was still dark], the Cowboys took us into a big field at the bottom of a hill where there were a couple of big trees and told us to wait for them. They said: "Don't move. Don't go anywhere. Stay right here."

Most of us were scared to death. We encouraged each other by saying things like, "Hang in there," and "You can do it. We've made it this far. We've gone through tap-in and we've gone through the semester. Let's hang in there and finish it up."

After hours of waiting, it began to turn daylight and suddenly, from out of nowhere, we heard a clicking noise... like boards clicking together. It started in the distance, then became louder and louder.

The sound came from the top of the hill several hundred yards in both directions. "The picture in my mind was of Indians coming over the hill."

Then all the Oldmen Cowboys appeared. They were each hitting two paddles together as they came over the hill. They started to whoop and yell as the clicking became louder until they became unified and stood together at the top of the hill overlooking us.

At the sign of one of the leaders, the Cowboys ran down the hill toward us. They drew three large circles on the ground and told us to "circle up" around those three circles.

We were told to bend over with our rear ends facing the outside of the circle. We were to look at each other's faces. There were seven in each circle so we were spread out enough that there was plenty of room for the Cowboys to swing their paddles.

We were told, "Put your hands on your ankles and look up. Don't move. Grab your pants and don't let go. If you let go of your pants, you're going to get hit, or beat, or you're going to get the cattle prod".

They began hitting us with one-handled paddles, each one taking three swings at each of us, then moving on to the next guy. Each round lasted five to ten minutes and seemed like an eternity.

A whistle blew and we would run over to a big oak tree they labeled "base," possibly a hundred yards away, up the side of the hill. We were allowed three to five minutes to recuperate between rounds.

A lot of these guys [Newmen pledges] were just anesthetized, drunk and stumbling. We were having to pick them up and pull them over to the base. I mean, they were crying. Some of the guys were bawling, just whining. I've never in my life heard so much stuff. We would say to each other, "We've got to make it through this. We've got to make it through this. We've got to get through the picnic, no matter what else is ahead."

So after three to five minutes, the whistle blew again and we went back and got another round.

If they hadn't gotten to you yet, they'd come to get you ... to get swings at you. The goal was for everybody to swing at everybody, to paddle and whip every Newman. So that's what they did.

Basically, we were all on the ground, on our knees, beat and crying. I remember guys putting their hands behind them, getting their hands beat up and yelling ... and – I've never seen anything like it in my life.

In between the paddlings, there were games that we would play. My group had to put tires around their heads and race in lines of two. The Cowboys would run alongside us saying, "Go, go, go." And as we ran up the hill, we were cattle prodded and paddled and eggs were thrown at us. At the top of the hill, we had to run around a tire, run back to the line and throw the tire to the next guy. We would get a minute or two before we would have to do it again. That went on two or three times.

Another time in between paddlings, the Cowboys lined us up and threw eggs at us. We would try to catch the eggs on our heads.

And God, I hated that cattle prod.

This went on over a period of about two hours ... until, finally, blood ran down our legs into our boots. Then everyone hugged and congratulated each other for becoming a Texas Cowboy.

We were told, "Man, you're a Cowboy. You made it! You're awesome! You're the best. You're cool." ⁷

For a long time, Watson thought the Cowboys' Motto was: "The rougher the initiation, the more close-knit the group." It was years later before he found out that their motto was: "Give your best to Texas and the best will come back to you." ⁸

On May 3, 1985 in an article in the *Daily Texan* regarding the Cowboys' initiation, Scott Scarborough said, "You got big guys swinging paddles, and they are swinging hard. You don't walk very well; you don't feel it until the next morning when your rear swells up. You don't turn over too many times while you're trying to sleep."

The 1987 Presidential Committee on Fraternal Organizations at University of Texas also found that the most serious effects from paddlings are often not realized for days. "Sometimes the blood drains from your butt into your testicles and really makes them swell up," one Silver Spur initiate said in the same article. [The Silver Spurs are a spirit group fraternity who takes care of Bevo, UT's Longhorn mascot. For years they did their *tap-in* the same evening as the Cowboys did, then afterwards they had a party together to celebrate].

"Many people bleed. They bleed through their blue jeans," Scarborough said. "The argument is if you go through tough times together, you'll stick together. Bull. There's no way you're developing camaraderie for those guys," he said. ⁸

Scarborough recalled having bleeding and swelling of the buttocks and a sense of deep humiliation. ⁹

Jim Hawley was paddled at least 50 times for his *tap-out* at the initiation-picnic he participated in, which took place the following morning. He admitted that it took him a month to recover. During Mr. Hawley's initiation in 1963, they had to run around carrying doors on their heads and had Tabasco poured on them. They had to walk through briar bushes and some people were required to jump into the lake. He was also cattle-prodded. ¹⁰

After it was all over, Scott Scarborough said: "I thought I was going to die. I kept thinking I was going through this so that nobody else would ever have to go through this." ¹¹

THE REAL ISSUES

In 1985, Scarborough invited Howard Richards, a member of the Board of Regents and a former Cowboy, to give a speech to the Cowboys about responsibility and not conducting or condoning hazing. Richards told the Cowboys that hazing was against the law and that things were different now. He asked them to quit hazing and said that he pledged that hazing would stop. When he left the room the Cowboys laughed, having no intention of stopping hazing.

After the *Daily Texan's* article on May 3, 1985, both Watson and Scarborough were ridiculed by many Cowboys, receiving phone calls from Cowboys who said, "You're going about it the wrong way," to which Scarborough responded, "We've tried it within the organization and no one's listening, and someone's going to get hurt. We don't want someone's injury or even death on our conscience."

Scarborough, a graduate student at UT, denounced hazing and denounced the Cowboys for doing it. Basically, he admitted, "We [Watson and Scarborough] were not the most popular Cowboys at this point and I was getting less interested in attending meetings."

He thought the most frustrating thing about all of this was that "we worked hard to do the right thing – to work with people within the organization." After Howard Richard's speech, he said, "You could just tell that things were not going to change."

"For a young man of 19," Lance Watson said, "the peer pressure of becoming a Cowboy and wanting to make it through the ordeal of pledging no matter what happened, even if it required doing whatever someone asked them to do, was overwhelming.

"Because of all that was going on, if they had asked you to jump off a cliff, you would have jumped off. You do what you're being told, 'Don't buck the system,' and 'Do what you're asked,' and I did that."

Watson said he loved being a Cowboy. But he really had a hard time appreciating their "traditions."

When asked what he thought about Gabe's death, Watson, now a Southern Baptist minister, said that he immediately suspected hazing and wrongdoing.

Scott Scarborough never attended any more Cowboy functions after the article in the *Daily Texan* because of his bitter feelings, shared with many past and current Cowboy members. He lost respect for what should and could have been a good organization and still feels very strongly against hazing. It was not what he had expected the highly respected group to do or even be associated with. [11]

Jake Fisher, who experienced pledging the Cowboys a few years before, thinks they still brand and believes that the brand is still around. "Guys can get their boots branded if they want to."

Jake said he had heard from a Silver Spur that they were making them swim across the river. This same friend said that they got a call from the President of the Texas Cowboys telling them to keep quiet about everything. He added that it was obvious to everyone that the guys out there were very drunk and that they were forced into the river by the Texas Cowboys, and that the guys were talking openly about being quiet if the cops called. [12]

Jim Hawley admitted that he no longer held the organization in esteem. "Once I went through the initiation, there was nothing there."

Hawley felt that part of the problem started years ago when universities all around the country took the housemothers and chaperones away, which left no one in charge. He felt Gabe's death was "blind negligence."

"When something has gone on so long, you can't stop it until it is so horrible that [a death] is the only way to stop it. It's gone on now for 35-40 [or more!] years. It was going on when I was there, so it's hardly a random act of a group that was out of control.

"When you have 20 or 21-year-olds looking at 18-year-olds and you're requiring them to slug down a lot of beer, it's inevitable: you have an accident ready to happen." [13]

ANONYMOUS LETTER

In 1987, William Cunningham, the President of University of Texas at that time, received an anonymous letter, written by the father of a Cowboy. This father talked about his son's beatings at the hands of the Cowboys, which left his son swollen, black and blue and scarred. He explained that they used double fisted paddles, and became "so intoxicated that they had no way of knowing how hard they were hitting the inductees." Also, they took "running starts before striking their bent-over targets with an unbelievable amount of force, usually causing them to throw up and bleed ... Eventually their flesh looked like raw meat after sustaining at least thirty strikes."

This father was concerned about the "traditions" the pledges were forced to endure which jeopardized their health and life. "Somehow tradition pales in light of the serious injuries that could result from one misplaced blow. Whether it is one's spine, thigh, or backside, it seems senseless to risk maiming someone, or worse."

The letter told why the father had sworn secrecy to his son, "making it impossible for me to sign this letter." He said it was because his son felt that "should anyone discover that I have written to you, [my son] would never work in the state of Texas."

He continued with a request, "I trust that you shall make your concerns known to both The Spurs and The Cowboys and put my worst fears to rest. My son's scars will remain with him for life. Thank God he only has scars."

President Cunningham's response to this letter was to send it to the police, the Vice President of UT, and to several parents with the following statement attached: "Anonymous letters and calls don't qualify."

COMMENTS

This happened years ago and maybe University of Texas' stance has changed since then. Yet one has to wonder why even an anonymous letter like the one above didn't kick in some kind of action against the Texas Cowboys, or at the very least an investigation. But it didn't.

Maybe if it had, just maybe, Gabe might still be alive.

~15~

WHO'S SON WILL BE NEXT?

In November of 1994, six months before Gabe's death, University of Texas President Robert Berdahl met with the Texas Cowboys, the Silver Spurs, and the Greek fraternity leaders and told them "hazing must stop or someone was going to die." [1,2]

"Well, a young man is now dead," President Berdahl said after Gabe died. [2]

"The death has 'the earmarks' of a hazing incident," University of Texas' President Berdahl said as he left Higgins' funeral. [2,3]

On Wednesday, May 3, 1995, hundreds of somber young men and women gathered at Gabe's memorial service.

"He was really friendly, really into his fraternity. He really loved his fraternity. He was just a friendly, fun guy to hang around with. I can't believe he's gone. I keep asking where is he."

"Gabe was a very nice individual, a very good friend. He was just a good person. We all loved Gabe."

"Gabe was a real good natured, very likable guy. [His death] really just put things in perspective. It made me realize again how precious every day is with the people you come in contact with."

"The incomprehensible question of 'Why?' keeps entering my mind."

"Gabe was a shy, gentle child," said his father. "He came to UT, and he blossomed."

"To me, Gabe was one of the best," said a Kappa Sigma fraternity brother.

"If there was something that's against the law, it's terrible to waste a person this young. You raise a child; you send a child to a school like the University of Texas, and then something like this happens," Lt David Campos, the investigating officer said. "Parents believe that their family members are in your hands when they attend the University." [4,5]

THE INVESTIGATIONS

The police investigation began Monday morning as soon as the Bastrop County Sheriff read in the paper that it had been a fraternity initiation. Led by Lt. David Campos, the office was inundated with 15 to 20 tips a day, mostly from college students who wanted to remain anonymous. One such caller said, "They were swimming because the Cowboys had a fire on the other side of the river and the Newmen were supposed to swim across and put it out after drinking." [4]

Many of the students I talked with agreed that they had been told that it was part of the initiation that the pledges were told to swim across the river. Other sources said similar things, but the police said they couldn't do anything about them until someone with a name came forward.

Besides the Bastrop County Sheriff's investigation, other investigations were conducted by the University of Texas Dean of Students, the Texas Alcoholic Beverage Commission, and The Texas Rangers, who were called in to assist the Bastrop County Sheriff's investigation.

The problem was that no one really knew the truth about what happened because no one in the fraternity was talking. "Hazing can be difficult to crack and prosecute," Assistant Attorney Kate Kelly in the Travis County District Attorney's Office said. "They have the best closed-mouth system I've ever seen," she said, referring to fraternities. [4]

Lt. Compos commented, "These guys are supposedly the pillars of society or the potential pillars of society. Apparently, no one's conscience is bothering them." [5]

Both the university's investigation and the police investigation gave the pledges immunity, hoping they would step forward and tell the truth. "I realize that some of these pledges may feel that if something illegal was going on that they [would] be responsible," Lt. Campos said. The pledges "are not being looked at as having violated the law. We are just looking for someone to tell the truth." [6]

UT's investigation began by interviewing each of the sixteen [Oldmen] Cowboys that were present during the "picnic," the ten Cowboys who arrived the next morning and the 29 Newmen/pledges who were there.

Written statements from each of those young men were required by the Bastrop Sheriff's investigation. Six of them refused to produce any statements with no penalties.

CODE OF SILENCE

Friday, May 12th, the newspapers reported that for nearly two weeks, the investigation of Gabe's death had been stalled by a traditional code of silence often maintained by Greek fraternities. UT's President Robert Berdahl said that he was promising a "thorough, detailed" investigation and added that previous investigations had been stymied due to this code of silence.

"I have publicly compared hazing to gang activity in that it is a violent activity, illegal and the participants become co-conspirators covering their illegal acts by observing a code of silence," President Berdahl said. [2]

While some believed that speculation of hazing was unfair, others thought that it would only lead to a "slap on the wrist." [2]

"The University will not do anything at all to embarrass or call attention to these young men," said a UT employee. "Hazing is still rampant within the organization. The fraternities are out of control. That, I guess, is an acceptable risk for UT administrators." [2]

On Saturday, May 13th, the papers reported, prematurely, that the web of silence about the case was beginning to crack. "There are rumblings that people are wanting to talk," said Lt. David Campos, investigating officer from the Bastrop Sheriff's Office. [7]

Quite the opposite was true. No one was talking.

Assistant Attorney Kate Kelly said: "Definitions that involve intent could be the most difficult things to prove in court. The fraternities really band together when something bad happens. The pledges aren't going to say the fraternity made them do it, and the fraternity isn't going to talk." [8]

UT HAZING

A 1987 University of Texas presidential commission report on fraternal organizations, which is considered one of the most definitive looks at hazing, found that hazing at UT had "become increasingly infused with alcohol consumption."

The Texas Cowboys weren't the only fraternity to have the disturbing tradition of hazing. "The Cowboy/Spur custom at *tap-in* is particularly disturbing," it said.

The commission report found that "New members are tapped – invited to join the organization – by a committee of older members from the same social fraternity as the prospective new member. After the new member is tapped, the men often meet at a previously designated bar where they 'drink as fast as they can' before the hazing begins." [1]

Even though the 1987 UT Presidential Commission Report found that the Cowboys continue "to permit hazing in some of its most blatant and offensive forms," including paddling and using cattle prods, it added that many students believed that the Texas Cowboys were "no longer considered desirable." [4]

BOYS WILL BE BOYS

Texas has a tough hazing law, which is seldom, if ever, used to bring hazing cases to trial. Senator Gonzalo Barrientos, D-Austin, wrote the law in 1987. "I think in spite of the law, some people are saying boys will be boys."

Barrientos said he'd been angry for years at the lack of prosecution under the law he passed after the death of Mark Seeberger [hazing involving alcohol poisoning, 1986]. "It's disgusting to me that we put up with this crap," he said. [4]

The lawyer who represented the Seeberger family, E.G. Morris, said that regarding hazing, he thought: "Passing a law doesn't stop an act. It just criminalizes it." [5]

"Until college and university administrators, prosecutors, and law enforcement take this seriously, the law will mean nothing," said Senator Barrientos. [8]

The Texas hazing code is one of the best in the nation. The law makes causing "serious bodily injury" during an act of hazing a felony under state jurisdiction. Barrientos said in an interview after Gabe's death that little progress had been made in preventing hazing injuries.

"I hope not one more life is lost before people take this thing very seriously," he said. "Whose son is going to be next?" [8]

~16~

KICKED OFF CAMPUS

COWBOYS BANNED FIVE YEARS

After a six-week investigation by University of Texas, Dr. Sharon Justice, University Texas Dean of Students, announced on Monday, June 12th, 1995, that the Texas Cowboys were banned from the University of Texas campus for five years until the year 2000.

Her findings claimed that the Texas Cowboys were found guilty of hazing using the following methods:

1. The purchase and consumption of alcohol by underage initiates,
2. Calisthenics,
3. Tackling,
4. The paddling of a new member,
5. The ingestion of hot dogs covered with tobacco,
6. Participation in drinking races,
7. Holding an event that subjected members to unreasonable risk, and
8. Horn honking

This was the third time in three years that the Cowboys had been penalized for hazing or alcohol violations.

In 1993, the Cowboys were punished for alcohol violations at an initiation ceremony, and in 1994 they were put on probation for a year for a hazing violation involving paddling at the *tap-in,* which occurred the first week of February 1994. The group was placed on a year's probation from April 1994 through April 1995, explaining why they were on probation during the time of Gabe's death. [1]

The decision banned the group from campus fund raising and recruitment and its most well known activity: firing Smokey the Cannon at UT football games. It also meant that the Cowboys were not allowed by the University to form "shadow organizations" to continue meeting under a different name, and they were required to submit new membership *tap-in* procedures that didn't involve hazing. [2]

Dr. Justice said she took into account that a five-year suspension could sink the group for good. But she said that the evidence supported a five-year penalty, during which time an entire class would enter and graduate from the University. [3]

CIVIL LAWSUIT

On Thursday, June 15, 1995, we filed a civil lawsuit.

The Cowboys and their lawyers continued to claim no wrongdoing: "Tragic though it is, Gabe Higgins' drowning was accidental and not the result of hazing," said Houston lawyer Michael Perrin, President of the newly formed Alumni of the Texas Cowboys, Inc. [4]

COWBOYS APPEAL FIVE-YEAR PENALTY

Friday, June 23, 1995, the Texas Cowboys appealed the five-year banishment from the UT campus, earlier announced on June 12th, which stated: "We are appealing the whole decision. The conclusions reached in the June 12th letter are fundamentally wrong," said Randy Leavitt, the Cowboys' lawyer. [5]

"Frankly, I think there is some basis for appealing," Perrin said. "What do you do with the scholarships? What do you do with the money raised for the ARC [Austin Retarded Citizens]?" Perrin formed the association to help the Cowboys regroup after the five-year penalty. [6]

WHAT MONEY?

The Texas Cowboys Alumni Association was formed the end of May 1995, only weeks after Gabe died. The remaining money that the pledges had raised that semester was shifted into a corporate Texas Cowboy Alumni account, which was now used to defend the young men who were listed in the civil lawsuit.

When we sued the Texas Cowboys in the Civil Law Suit, they only replied that they had no money, which was true. It was now in another account.

THE APPEAL
On Friday, July 21st, the Cowboys met behind closed doors (our lawyers were not permitted to attend) before Gaylord Jentz, a business law professor at UT who was appointed by the University as an appeals officer. The hearing was kept secret at the Cowboys' request, upheld by the University because the evidence included private student records.

Randy Leavitt, the Cowboys' lawyer, said he did not believe hazing occurred at the picnic and added, "I do not believe the facts constitute a hazing violation," he said. "We're hoping to get a fair resolution of the facts." [7]

THREE-YEAR PENALTY
Monday, July 24th, the hearing officer, Gaylord Jentz made a ruling upholding seven of the eight alleged hazing violations [mentioned earlier] against the Texas Cowboys. Jentz ruled that the Cowboys had committed three violations:

1. Instructing underage members to buy alcohol,
2. Encouraging them to participate in "drinking races," and
3. Holding an event that subjected members to unreasonable risk.

The other four that were dismissed involved calisthenics, eating hot dogs covered with tobacco, paddling a new member, and tackling in an ambush-like prank. The last one he didn't consider a serious allegation was the horn honking. [8, 9]

Thursday, July 27th, due to Jentz' decision, the university announced that the Cowboys' suspension had been shortened to three years plus one additional year of probation. [10, 11]

Randy Leavitt, legal counsel for the Cowboys, still found the penalty to be "harsh," commenting that "The drowning was a tragic accident but has absolutely nothing to do with hazing." [12]

TEXAS COWBOYS' HISTORY
Friday, July 28th, a Rap Sheet Editorial written by Chris Parry appeared in the *Daily Texan* supporting Dr. Justice's five-year suspension of the

Cowboys, stating the following:

The University needs to crack down on this rogue organization. First-time offenses might merit a lighter sentence. But the Cowboys have a history of abusing initiates.

1. *1931–1939. According to the Presidential Commission of Fraternal Organizations, the Cowboys branded initiates' chests throughout this era.*
2. *1940s and 1950s. A former Cowboys' pledge trainer, Scott Lange, claimed that the group continued to brand initiates throughout these decades. After being on probation in 1954, they cleaned up their act: they quit branding, began doing community service, and relabeled their "Hell Night" initiations: "Picnic."*
3. *1976.* <u>*The Daily Texan*</u> *sent a photographer to a Cowboys gathering at Pease Park. Cowboys' president Wayne Clearwater was photographed with a cattle prod in his hand. The University suspended the group for a month following the incident. [Picture enclosed]*
4. *1983. Scott Scarborough, President of the UT student body, claims to have been paddled and shocked with a cattle prod during his initiation. Two years later, he told his story to the Texan. "Many people bleed," he said. "They bleed through their blue jeans."*
5. *1985. In a Texan story, ex-Cowboy Lance Watson claimed that in the past an initiate was paddled so hard that his spleen ruptured and the initiate almost died.*
6. *1987. The Presidential Commission of Fraternal Organizations issued its report: "The University Administration has repeatedly warned the Texas Cowboys and the Silver Spurs to discontinue all hazing of all new members. Both organizations continue to permit hazing...including rides, paddling and use of electrical shocking devices." According to the Texan, the commission received several reports of Cowboy initiates who suffered swollen and bleeding testicles from excessive paddling.*
7. *1994. The Cowboys were suspended from the first three football games after they were cited for paddling initiates. Dean Justice said, "We determined that pledges had been blindfolded, hit, punched, paddled and required to participate in calisthenics and lineups."* [13]

THREE-YEAR RULING APPEALED

On August 4th, Dr. Sharon Justice appealed the three-year ruling to reinstate the five-year penalty. [14]

FIVE-YEAR PENALTY REINSTATED

September 14th Dr. James Vick ruled to reinstate the Cowboys' five-year suspension.

"I feel that it was the appropriate punishment," Vick said. "The University is seriously committed to ending hazing, and it is prepared to raise the penalties for groups who repeatedly violate those hazing regulations." Vick said he reinstated the harsher penalty because of the Cowboys' past hazing violations.

"Even though five years is a significant step, it certainly seems insignificant compared to the life of Gabe Higgins," my attorney, Jeff Rusk, said. "Five years of not blowing off a cannon is hardly a punishment." [15]

GRAVESTONE CARTOON

September 7th, the Daily Texas ran a cartoon of two Cowboys looking at Gabe's headstone marker. One Cowboy says to the other, "Suspended for three whole years, can you believe it?" [16] [See Picture]

2ND GRAVESTONE CARTOON

The same day the news of the five-year penalty being reinstated was released, the Daily Texan ran the same "Gravestone Cartoon" of the two Cowboys looking at Gabe's grave, with a different inscription. The comment was changed to, "Actually, I think they just made it five years again." [17] [See Picture]

EDITORIALS

'What cattle prod?'

Members of the Cowboys, an honorary social and service organization, emerge from the woods with cattle prods after a "gathering" at Pease Park Thursday. When asked the purpose of the prods, Cowboy president Wayne Clearwater responded, "I didn't see any cattle prods," and claimed that the Cowboys don't haze their members. "We blindfolded them and walked them down to a campfire. We have our private ceremony. That's all there is to it."

—Texan Staff Photo by Ted Henshaw

COMMENTARY ON GRAVESTONE CARTOON

So many comments were received at the Daily Texan on the Gravestone Cartoon that on September 18th the editor, Robert Rogers, wrote an article stating that the cartoon suggested: "misplaced priorities," and that the cartoonist sought to dramatize the "inappropriateness of the Cowboys' attempts to dodge even a relatively mild punishment for the death of their friend."

He continued: *Does criticizing the Cowboys' attempt to escape a rightful punishment insult Higgins' memory? Absolutely not. Quite the contrary, the best way to honor Gabe Higgins would be to stop the activities that killed him.*

The real insult to Higgins' memory is that his Cowboy companions would spend so much time and effort finagling to escape punishment for their misdeeds. The Cowboys and their lawyers, not the Texan's cartoonist, are the ones who trivialize Higgins' death.

The death of Higgins was not a freak accident, a one-in-a-million chance occurrence. Instead, it was the predictable result of a well-entrenched campus tradition of irresponsible drinking and violating Texas laws against hazing.

Whenever students engage in dangerous activities like binge drinking, or perilous stunts, the risk of injury or death is always present. If for years students are coerced into dangerous activities, it is only a matter of time before someone gets hurt or killed. [18]

CIVIL LAWSUIT

August 31, 1995 we sued the Texas Cowboys organization, six officers, and the Bastrop County landowner, alleging that the group's initiation-picnic was the culmination of hazing activities, which began in February when Gabe was "tapped in" and was "physically whipped, beaten, and struck" as part of the tap-in ritual. [19]

SMOKEY THE CANNON

Before school started that fall, there began a heated debate about who would be the new sponsor of Smokey the Cannon. Dr. Sharon Justice had stated that it didn't matter how many years Dr. Vick decided to suspend the Cowboys, she was firm in her delivery that they would not be allowed on the football field to shoot Smokey the Cannon any time soon.

Since Smokey the Cannon belonged to the Cowboys and hadn't been used since 1986, people went looking for the old cannon. They found it in storage in the Memorial Stadium where it had been for kept for eight years. The old cannon had been built with a sawed-off shotgun inside the shell. When they opened it up, they found that someone had taken the sawed-off shotgun! Since sawing off a shotgun was illegal, replacing it became a problem. To do so would have required a federal permit to use it. [20]

HISTORY OF SMOKEY

The Texas Cowboys presented the original University of Texas cannon to the University in 1954. Thanks to the antics of some Texas A&M students, the original cannon is at the bottom of Town Lake. The Cowboys and alumni replaced the cannon with Smokey II in the fall of 1968. In 1974, Smokey II was donated to the University and construction of Smokey III [the Cowboys' present cannon] began.

Both Smokey III and its trailer are authentic replicas of Civil War artillery, handcrafted in Tennessee and Austin. The cannon stands six feet tall, ten feet long and weighs more than 1,000 pounds. It is equipped to fire four 10-gauge shells at once. The $15,000 price tag of the trailer and gun was raised through the donations of past and present Cowboys. [21]

SILVER SPURS GET SMOKEY

September 15, 1995 the Silver Spurs contracted a five-year lease with the Cowboys for the genuine and current "Smokey" to carry on the tradition of shooting the cannon at the football games during the five years the Cowboys were not permitted on the field. [22]

GRAND JURY "NO BILLS" CRIMINAL CHARGES

February 8th, 1996, after an hour of testimony and fifteen minutes of deliberation (our lawyers weren't allowed to attend), the Grand Jury returned with a decision not to charge any members of the Texas Cowboys with criminal wrongdoing.

"The criminal investigation ended after the grand jury was asked to focus on reckless conduct and manslaughter," Lt. David Campos said. The only thing that could reopen it is "substantial new evidence," Bastrop County District Attorney Charles Penick said.

When told about the grand jury's "no bill" on the criminal lawsuit, the reaction from Jack Price, Gabe's father's lawyer was, "The only people involved were the Cowboys ... and they weren't going to incriminate themselves. Of course, Gabe Higgins wasn't there to speak. It was probably a rough thing for the district attorney to present." [23,24,25]

RELEASE OF UT'S INVESTIGATION

February 19th, 1996, the Cowboys wanted to block the release of the University of Texas' investigation documents, claiming that the student records should be kept private.

Scott Young, an attorney for the Cowboys said, "Student information other than directory information is not supposed to be released."

My lawyer, Jeff Rusk, stated that the investigation results did not fall under the student privacy laws. "Illegal acts are not something that is protected," Rusk said.

Though the records were considered student records, the University stated that they would release them under subpoena. [26]

The University of Texas was subpoenaed, and a judge order ruled that UT was to disclose the investigation information [to my knowledge, that meant *all* of it]. Yet there was no record of the question/answer interrogation part of UT's investigation in the file when I received it a year later.

The Daily Texan editor Robert Rogers comments were:

"This may be a wise legal maneuver.[to block the release of the files]. *If we were representing the Cowboys, we certainly would try to suppress any information about the Cowboys' role in activities that could have contributed to the death of UT student Gabe Higgins.*

"But however wise a legal tactic, keeping that information secret is against the public interest. The Texas Cowboys were – and still are to some, a respected bunch. If the Cowboys did not cause or contribute to Higgins' death, UT students need to know so the Cowboys can clear their much-soiled name. If, on the other hand, the Cowboys did cause or contribute to the death of a UT student, the public deserves to have that information to form an opinion on this organization." [27]

Shortly after that article appeared in the *Daily Texan*, on the last day of February, the Bastrop Sheriff's Department's investigation became available to the public.

On Sunday, March 3rd, 1996, Mary Ann Roser wrote an extensive article on this case from that file. Excerpts are in next chapter. [28]

TWELVE MORE SUED

On April 23, 1996, almost a year after Gabe died, we sued twelve more Texas Cowboys in the civil lawsuit. The lawsuit now named 17 active Cowboy members, including twelve officers and five other Cowboys who were present that night. It also named the pledge who suggested the late-night swim, the landowner, and the Texas Cowboys organization. The total sued were 19 individuals plus the Texas Cowboys. [29,30]

THE SETTLEMENT

The end of January 1997, after two full days of depositions, Tim (Gabe's dad) and I decided to settle out of court.

We were both overwhelmed and discouraged that they kept implying their total innocence, labeling what happened an accident and placing any and all blame and responsibility on Gabe for his participation and drinking during the evening of the picnic. Neither of us could deal with the thought of going through a trial.

The Cowboys' homeowner's policies paid for this lawsuit. We dismissed the Cowboy officer who had no insurance yet was one of the top five most responsible for the hazing. Those five had to take their senior year over again and do some community service. As for the Texas Cowboys organization, they were not permitted back on campus for five years.

We did not sue the University of Texas. Doing so would have been regarded a "frivolous lawsuit" because UT has been deemed with sovereign immunity by the Texas Legislature with three exceptions: (1) any accidents on their property, (2) any accidents in any of their vehicles, (3) any malpractice by any of their medical doctors. Our lawsuit didn't line up under any of those criteria and even though I requested it of my lawyer, he wouldn't sue them.

~17~

LORD OF THE FLIES

The literal translation of "Beelzebub" is Satan, Prince of the devils, and *Lord of the Flies*.

Matthew 12:24, 27; Luke 11:15

"Never mind what's sense. That's gone." [Eric said to Ralph]

Lord of the Flies by William Golding 1

Evil is present in us all, and we must struggle not to allow it to dominate us. Like all of humanity, these boys have and act on impulses that are at best uncivil and at worst deadly.

Goldberg's Cliff Notes on *Lord of the Flies*

The book Lord of the Flies is about a plane full of young British boys that crashes on an island, killing the pilot and the co-pilot. It's a story of survival and reveals how the "inherent evil that dwells in each of us can rise up, savagely attack, and eventually kill selected individuals who do not fit into the group." (Cliff Notes)

After Gabe's funeral, I turned to my mother and remarked, "Doesn't this whole thing sound like what happened in *Lord of the Flies*?"

She responded: "Yeah, but the fellow at the end of that book doesn't die." The rescue plane lands on the beach just as the "tribe" of young twelve year old boys run after one of the boys in the group with clubs, savagely intent on killing him.

Whether or not this scenario can be pinned on the Texas Cowboys the night Gabe died is not my goal. Pointing out the haunting similarities is.

During the course of the lawsuit in the spring of 1997, I had lunch a few times with Dr. Sharon Justice, Dean of Students at University of Texas. It was during one of those times I asked her why the University of Texas hadn't kept closer tabs on the Cowboys if they knew they were so wild and were known to practice hazing.

She answered, "Ruth, we have over 700 organizations at UT. We can't keep tabs on all of them." She continued, "Yesterday I received a phone call from a UT alumna, the mother of a young lady in one of the sororities. She told me to 'lay off' the sororities. 'After all, we drank when we went to college and we turned out all right. That's what college is all about.' Then she told me to 'Back off.'"

It was at that moment that I decided to be the squeaky wheel and write this book. It also made me wonder who was running the show if the alumni were calling the shots.

WHO TO BELIEVE

Either the Cowboys' story is true or it isn't. It was either "just an unfortunate accident," like they said, or it wasn't.

It's my opinion that the whole truth about what happened to Gabe unfortunately never came out in the lawsuit or in any of the investigations. It's also my opinion that it wasn't "just an unfortunate accident."

Before I explain, please read the following excerpts from the March 3, 1996, issue of the *Austin American-Statesman* written by Mary Ann Roser, which she gathered from the newly released police files:

> *Members of the Cowboys and their lawyers said the truth is in the statements given to the sheriff's department and UT officials. They make up most of the investigation's 2079 pages and are similar because "There is only one truth," said Cliff Condrey, a Cowboys' pledge. He claimed it was his idea to defy the active Cowboys' order to stay away from the river.*

> *For the Cowboys and pledges, the grand jury vindicated what they have said all along: Higgins' death was a tragic accident, and no one was to blame.*

> *But a lie detector test given to Condrey showed deception when he said it was his idea alone for Higgins to go swimming. It showed deception again*

when he answered 'no' to the question: "Are you intentionally lying to cover up for the Cowboys?"

"The whole notion of the conspiracy of silence infuriated me," Condrey said. "We went out of our way to give very detailed statements to the authorities and the university. This was the loss of a young man's life due to nobody's calling but God's ... There was nothing in the world that we could have done other than not be there."

Condrey continued: "I never thought he drowned until they pulled him out," adding that he deeply regretted suggesting the swim. "Had I thought one of my friends was drowning, I would have done anything in my power to stop that from happening."

Most of the Cowboys said that they did not consider the activities at the picnic to be hazing, according to Dean of Students Sharon Justice.

"I told the truth about everything," said John Welsh [Gabe's pledge mate], who was there that night and knew Higgins best. "Otherwise, I could not live with anything as important as my close friend dying."

MY COMMENTS:

The conspiracy of silence was devastating. I always held out that at least one of the young men would step forward and tell the truth about what happened that night. It didn't happen.

Gabe's death wasn't "just an accident," or "the loss of a young man's life due to nobody's calling but God's." The truth is that it was due to gross negligence of the entire system. Afterwards, everyone seemed to look the other direction as if no one was guilty. It was all too convenient to blame Gabe because he wasn't around to tell what really happened.

An innocent life was lost! If this is the price of initiation, then it's too high! If this is the game they play, or require their pledges to play, then why isn't someone somewhere doing something to stop it?

Most of what the Cowboys reported in their statements, regarding what happened before midnight, I believe, was true with two exceptions:

1. Mad Dog20/20. The Cowboys state they required the Newmen to bring one bottle of Mad Dog 20/20 each, or 30 bottles. However,

the list that was handed to Newman John True that Wednesday night required the Newmen to bring 60 bottles, which is two bottles per pledge. I believe that 60 bottles were purchased and taken to the initiation-picnic, not 30. (I have the actual list in my possession.)

2. Forced Drinking. None of the Cowboys admitted there was any forced drinking. Yet it was a well-known fact that the Cowboys practiced forced drinking on their pledges through the semester.

Primarily, I question everything that the Cowboys said happened *after* midnight when the pledges went back to their camp for the last time. There are too many flaws in their stories. It made me totally doubt their accounts of what happened that night *after* the Newmen went back to their campfire.

The following points list the discrepancies and flaws in their stories:

1. The Tap-in Paddling. The Cowboys were on probation for paddling from the year before. How in the world did they get away with paddling the pledges for *tap-in* while they were still on probation? How did it get past UT when the University had full knowledge of this "tradition?" Why did UT continually look the other direction and allow the Cowboys to still practice hazing without holding them accountable? It makes me question how tolerant UT is/was of hazing.

2. The lie detector test taken by Cliff Condrey. The four questions that indicated deception were:
Q: Did anyone plan for Gabe to go in the water? A: No
Q: Are you intentionally lying in your statement to cover-up for the Cowboys? A: No
Q: Was it your idea for Gabe to go swimming with you? A: Yes
Q: Do you know for sure if anyone else suggested that Gabe go swimming in the river? A: No
What was he covering up?

3. The code of silence. Reports surfaced from the Kappa Sigs and others that Carl Branson called the presidents of other fraternities, telling them to be quiet and not to talk to the police. The flurry of stories that came directly from the Cowboys themselves immediately after Gabe's death was suddenly silenced to nothing. If they were telling the truth, why the cover up? Why the weekly

meetings? And why wasn't UT more aggressive in their investigation? Why didn't they pursue what actually happened on the river? They didn't even question the young men a second time.

4. <u>The testimonies of the former Cowboys in Chapter 14</u>. These testimonies pose substantial evidence that hazing, paddling, cattle prodding, and forced drinking were deeply rooted in the Cowboys' tradition and that it was normal behavior to cover up their hazing practices, which include: the *tap-in* and *tap-out* (initiation-picnic), and the entire semester of hazing.

5. <u>Grant Granger's statement</u>. He said he thought there were "15 cases of beer" at the initiation and "about 20 bottles of Mad Dog." He also said he didn't know of anyone getting any tobacco on his hot dog. He was the pledge captain, in charge of the initiation-picnic and he didn't have any idea how much alcohol there was? He was the main cook and knew nothing about the tobacco-on-the-hot-dog thing?

6. <u>Carl Branson's statement</u>. He stated that he didn't think there were any "acts that would be interpreted as hazing in this ceremony." That statement was actually regarding the morning *tap-out* ceremony where the Cowboys traditionally paddled their Newman/pledges until blood ran into their boots. His statement also said that he did not see anyone chug any beers or be asked to do so. Many of the statements read contrary to that.

7. <u>They didn't call the police for almost ten hours</u> after Gabe disappeared.

8. <u>The campsites were meticulously cleaned up</u>. Isn't it against the law to destroy evidence at a crime scene?

9. <u>Texas Cowboy initiation or campout</u>? No one told the police that it was a fraternity party, or even a fraternity "picnic" when the police arrived at the campsite on Saturday at 12:30 p.m.

10. <u>The landowner's "deal"</u>. A year after the incident, the landowner met with his lawyer and my lawyer over lunch and proposed to my lawyer that if we would settle for the entire $100,000 insurance money, they would "come over on our side" and tell the whole truth that there was truckload after truckload of booze/beer taken onto the property. At that lunch meeting, Mr. Morgan admitted that he had a drink with the Cowboys early in the evening, which was quite opposite from what he stated in his interrogatories where

he not only denied having a drink with them, he denied seeing any alcohol. The "deal" didn't transpire because my ex-husband and his lawyer procrastinated in their decision to accept it. Mr. Morgan finally hired a lawyer to represent him and his portion of the settlement was $50,000. He never formally admitted to anything from that conversation.

11. <u>The Cowboys' clandestine meetings</u>. The Cowboys' officers met with lawyers within a couple hours after Gabe's body was pulled from the river, until midnight Saturday night. All of the Cowboys and pledges present at the initiation-picnic met for six hours the next day on Sunday, then later met a third time within a week after that at one of the fraternity houses. One statement said they met weekly after that. One can understand that these boys were experiencing grief. However, combined with a cover-up, one might assume that the reason they were meeting was to 1.Get their stories straight, and to 2. Get legal counsel. Their defense stated that they met to offer solace to the boys, which was true, but I don't believe that it was the entire truth.

12. <u>The keys</u>. The Newmen were required to hand over all their keys, wallets, belts, and watches early in the evening. They stated that the keys were taken to keep them from driving drunk on the ranch or "driving under the influence" on the highway. Question: Were the rest of the items collected to keep them from being ruined from the river water? If so, it would infer that the Oldmen planned for the Newmen to go into the water. One wonders why Newman John Welsh brought a change of clothes? Maybe he knew there was a chance he would be getting into the river?

13. <u>The pledge's mindset</u>. Two things happened when the keys were gathered up. It was a subliminal message of total control and one of the more blatant signs of the deadly trust that happens between pledges and actives. The Texas Cowboys initiation-picnic had been *tradition* for years. Everything they did was planned. Taking the keys and wallets conveyed to the Newmen that they could get drunk and wasted and it would be totally O.K. because this was "tradition;" it had been done before and the Oldmen "had everything under control."

Well, they didn't. Besides that, the statements revealed that most of them (referring to the Oldmen and the ones in charge) were stumbling drunk.

14. "Groupthink" mindset. The "groupthink" mindset of the pledges (explained in a later chapter) was deeply implanted by the time of the initiation. It's very similar to a victim's mindset. It took a semester of hazing to get this group of pledges pliable enough that they would do whatever they were told, just to make it through the final initiation. They were vulnerable subjects. They fully trusted the Oldmen. They were told to go back to their camp and that's what they did. After two nights of drinking, I believe that a trip to the river would only have happened if they were told to do that.

15. The paddling of one Newman. How believable is it that after the Newmen were sent back to their camp, the Cowboy officers were sitting around discussing whether or not they should paddle one pledge once *after* they had already paddled him? *And* when the plan was that they were going to excessively paddle them *all* until blood ran into their boots the following morning?

16. The probation. Part of the rules regarding the 1994 probation the year before was that the Cowboys were to have filed a document with UT stating that they would not be hazing their pledges at *tap-in*. All the officers signed it and gave it to the Dean's Office, yet they still paddled their pledges for *tap-in*. Another stipulation of the probation was that they were supposed to let the University know the time and place of any other initiations. Did they do this? If so, why wasn't this information released by UT?

17. The best defense is a good offense. They blamed Gabe for *his* negligence! Not only the statements, but also the interrogatories, the newspapers (mainly comments in the letters to the editor, most of them from Cowboys) and the lawyer who called the case a frivolous lawsuit, seemed to be brutal in their denial of any wrongdoing or any blame. According to them, Gabe's death was totally *his* fault because he was drinking and because the pledges were told not to go to the river.

18. Gabe was a good swimmer. I had a hard time figuring out how Gabe could have drowned in the first place. He was an excellent swimmer. That would also include the knowledge and proper re-

spect of the dangers of lakes, rivers, and the ocean. I've had many discussions with family and friends who have agreed with me that we couldn't imagine him being so stupid as to have gone swimming in the river, fully clothed, and drunk.

19. <u>Linking arms</u>. It doesn't make sense that they linked arms going down to the river. Even if they held onto each other's back pocket or something, a normal person doesn't walk through the woods that way unless they are told to do so in an organized fashion. Normal people need their arms to balance themselves and would not require holding onto the person ahead of them AND behind them. That would be a very uncomfortable way to walk anywhere! Especially at night over the terrain they had to walk through. Q: Were they told to do so?

20. <u>The water moccasin nest</u>. Most of these boys were Texans and had to have known of the danger of swimming in the water moccasin-infested waters around Austin. The water moccasin is an aggressive, poisonous snake that is prolific in the region. They should never have been in that river. It's amazing that none of them were bitten. The nest was between the sandbar and the shore of the Morgan Ranch, found by the team of men who dragged the river for Gabe's body.

21. <u>Fearless Cowboy tradition</u>. Everything done at the picnic involved great planning and was wrapped in tradition. A big part of being a Cowboy was all about facing physical danger with strength and no fear. Why did the former Cowboys in Chapter 14 believe that it was part of the initiation to have them swim the river? Because it was tradition. Hazing in any form during the initiation-picnic was tradition.

The following is a more probable scenario than the one that we've been led to believe by the Cowboys and is my opinion of what really happened:

After midnight of the initiation-picnic, the Newmen had been told it was over. They went back to their camp for the last time thinking they were done for the evening. They were sitting around their campfire, talking, "high-fiving" each other and happy they were done after a long semester of hard work. Some of the Oldmen walked up the hill to the Newmen's camp and after congratulating them for making it this far in the initiation, told them that they wanted to see if any of the Newmen were man enough to prove themselves worthy of becoming a most fearsome, awesome Cowboy: the tests of strength and endurance were about to begin. The Newmen responded with whoops and hollers. Then the Oldmen, the OLDMEN (NOT the Newmen) led them to the river, to "seal their boots onto their feet." Another tradition.

22. <u>Fighting on the river</u>. Why in the world would the Newmen be fighting on the river after being so happy and "high-five-ing" at the campfire? It's hard to imagine Gabe doing that. Maybe they were told to "Vie for Top Dog" or something. It doesn't connect that they should be "high-five-ing" at the campfire and congratulating each other, then minutes later fighting at the river! I can't imagine Gabe tearing the shirt off another pledge without wondering if he was fighting for his life. Gabe was an amiable and mellow, easy-going young man, especially when drinking. He was known to be a peacemaker. Before the code of silence set in, Cliff Condrey told one of the Kappa Sigs that they had yelled at Gabe and called him a "pussy" during the initiation. Did they verbally gang up on him at the river? What happened? What are they hiding? And why was there no investigation into this?

23. <u>Told to do so</u>. I believe that they were probably told to swim the river as a test of strength and endurance. If it were daylight, if the river weren't as wide as it was with ripples on top that revealed undercurrents, if the setting were in Idaho where there are no water moccasins, I might be willing to accept the idea that the pledges wanted to swim this huge wide river for recreation. Also, considering the "groupthink" and gang mentality, I can't see the pledges swimming the river after two nights of serious drinking, most of them drunk, in the pitch dark night, without being told to do so, or at the very least, being challenged to do so.

SO THEN, WHAT REALLY HAPPENED?

A. I ruled out a water moccasin bite, even though the nest was only about 15–25 feet from where they were on the sandbar. The poison from a bite would have shown up in the blood test and the Medical Examiner would have detected a bite on his skin. Besides, the autopsy definitely showed that he died of drowning (ie: the pink fluid).

B. I ruled out the possibility that he could have gotten cramps in the water from eating the hot dog. People can die from getting cramps if they go swimming too soon after they eat. The stomach will cramp and the person will double up in a ball unable to swim. If that had happened to Gabe, I imagine that he would have been close enough to call out to someone. A person will get those kinds of cramps within an hour after eating. The last of the Newmen ate more than an hour (or two) before they went into the water. The autopsy showed that Gabe's hot dog was partially digested. [Side Note: No tobacco was ingested].
C. I have questioned why they would have ganged up on him. Perhaps it was because he wasn't a Texan or even a southerner (even though he lived in Galveston one year). Maybe neither. Since the truth of what happened on the river was never revealed, it remains an unsettled, unanswered question.
D. It's incomprehensible that anyone could have deliberately held Gabe's head under. His drowning was not a hateful act of cruelty, but an act of negligence and stupidity. These were a group of guys who were the cream of the crop, good guys from good families. I have honestly never entertained this scenario.
E. The reports from the boys said that Gabe didn't swim the river.
F. The only remaining, feasible possibility would be that they threw him in. Everyone was drunk, running around wild and crazy, fighting to the point of tearing someone's shirt off.

The most probable scenario that I believe happened is this:

I can see Gabe in the dark, moonless night, walking to the point furthest down river on the sandbar, away from all the noise. He stops, facing away from them, resting his hands on his hips, frustrated and angry because he'd worked so hard for them all semester. He had been told the initiation-picnic would be a fun, easy time. They had already thrown him in the water several times. They had called him names. Foul names. Many of them were still drunk. I see him disconnecting, walking away from them seeking some area of sanity amidst the noise and chaos.

Then in the darkness, three or four of them grab him from behind, tackle him, pick him up and throw him into the river, walking off, and in their drunkenness, not turning around to see if he came back up.

The reason why I believe he walked to the point farthest down river on the sandbar is because they found his body 50 yards (150 feet) down river from where the young men were and even in a river of that size, I am told, a drowning victim's body would only move about 75 feet In the water.

In the *Daily Texan* on September 14, 1995, both Dr. Vick and Dr. Justice admitted that the UT investigation did NOT focus on Gabe's death. Their investigation focused on the hazing and drinking that happened earlier in the night, such as: *where the Newmen purchased the alcohol, how much beer they bought, when they got there, the drinking games, the calisthenics, the eating of hot dogs: questions involving acts of hazing during the early part of the evening.* Any questions involving what happened on the river were not pursued.

None of the young men present that night were questioned a second time, with the exception of Cliff Condrey, who took a lie detector test. Neither of the investigations ever interrogated any of Gabe's friends who knew about his being hazed for the *tap-in* and throughout the semester.

The Dean of Students office had been completely informed about the Cowboys' hazing practices traditionally carried out every semester, including minute details. They knew the Cowboy pledges were cattle prodded. They knew they were hazed throughout the semester. They knew they paddled their pledges for *tap-in* and *tap-out* because it was tradition and because they had received reports from dropouts like Jake Fisher, who dropped out before having to endure the initiation-picnic, and from concerned parents, like the anonymous letter.

My position remains that something very serious went wrong on the river that night that no one has admitted to or been held accountable for.

THE TRUTH

All I ever wanted to know was the truth about what happened, especially that night of the initiation.

After putting all the pieces of this puzzle together, I feel that they did not admit the truth and since they were not questioned again, I believe that the lies they told were eventually believed. I also believe that the punishment never fit the crime because the true crime was never revealed. My guess is that they were encouraged to keep their mouths shut, specifically about two things: leading the Newmen down to the water as part of the initiation and requiring or encouraging them to swim across the river.

Because a life was lost, it's likely that, had the truth prevailed, some of the Cowboys might have gone to prison. According to the law, that's what should have happened.

The basic problem with that is that had any of these young men gone to prison for this crime, their lives would have been totally ruined. Most of these young men, certainly the officers, were from influential, wealthy families, and for them to have been accused of this crime and sentenced such a powerful edict would have devastated everyone involved, including their families. The Texas Cowboys organization would have been permanently kicked off campus, their reputation darkened: tarnishing the Texas Cowboys' good name. (It *did* tarnish their name!) Plus, it certainly would have been a black eye on the University of Texas.

So it seems that it was in everyone's best interest to protect these young men and this organization from that devastation.

With one exception: Gabe lost his life.

So who defended Gabe?

After Gabe's death, Senator Barrientos, who was responsible for writing and implementing the state hazing code in 1987, which is one of the best-written anti-hazing laws in the nation, was quoted in the newspapers wondering why no one had ever used the law and why no one had ever been prosecuted in the state of Texas for hazing. He added that it made him upset that the laws were in place and he didn't know why they were not used. (They actually have been used, but no one had ever gone to prison in Texas at that point).

If you have enough money to hire a good enough lawyer quickly enough, and if you are willing to lie, most of the time you can skirt the crime, or at least try to. It happens all the time in America.

The Cowboys kept stating that it was a terrible accident and that it was only a "picnic" they attended, not an initiation. It took our lawyers a year and a half to get the Cowboys and their lawyers to even *admit* that the "picnic" was actually an initiation. We did so by providing a document that was presented to Gabe's father and myself at the viewing the night before Gabe's Memorial Service in Austin. It certifies that Gabe became a Member of the Texas Cowboys at the University of Texas at Austin, signed, dated, and labeled: "Date of initiation." [Document enclosed]

The truth is that Gabe's death was the product of many years of wrongful tradition. It was the result of many young men over a period of 60+ years living on the edge of being too wild and too crazy, and thinking that the way they carried on was acceptable behavior.

What it was, was abusive behavior at its worst.

One problem lies in the defining of who is at blame. Was it the boys who were there that night, the landowner, the alumni, the University of Texas, the whole Greek system, the Texas Cowboy organization, the parents, the lawyers, the individual students, the incompleteness of the investigations, or the mores of society? Or was it simply Gabe's fault?

My answer to that is that I think we're all to blame.

I've come full circle. Maybe there is an "inherent evil that dwells in each of us," a dark side of our nature that, given the right [or wrong] setting, "can rise up and savagely attack, and eventually kill individuals who do not fit into the group," similar to the book *Lord of the Flies*. In our civilized country and society, one has to question whether or not it is so civilized when things like this happen to good young men with great potential.

Three weeks after Gabe died, my oldest son, Brian graduated with a Ph.D. in Engineering. It was a bittersweet experience. Most of our extended family sat in the stands in tears as he was hooded. We were not only crying for joy for Brian after so many years of hard work, we were grieving over the potential that died with Gabe: the little brother that should have been part of this celebration. The little brother and son who lost it all, "just trying to belong."

~18~

THE TEXAS COWBOYS' REFORMATION

Early in the fall of 2000, I received an invitation to the University of Texas annual banquet for all the recipients and donors of scholarships for the coming school year held at the Lila B. Etta Alumni Center.

Funded by donations from the Texas Cowboys' Alumni organization, the first Texas Cowboy/ Gabriel Higgins Scholarship was awarded in September 2000 to its first recipient, sophomore Rupesh Patel, a member of the newly re-formed Texas Cowboys.

After a long five-year wait, the new Texas Cowboys had been birthed with thirty-five Cowboys who were scheduled to shoot the cannon at the first UT football game of the season on September 23, 2000.

During the banquet one of the two alumni officers I sat next to invited me to speak the next day at the Texas Cowboys Alumni Board meeting. It was held in one of those posh legal buildings on Congress Boulevard only a couple blocks from the capitol. I took the elevator to the 28th floor then took the second elevator to the 34th floor.

When I spoke to them, I thanked them for having such a powerful influence in the reformation of the new Cowboys and also for sponsoring the scholarship in Gabe's name. Then I encouraged and challenged these powerful, influential men to take a stand against hazing. I told them that they were in a strategic place to do so.

Two weeks later, there was an article in the paper announcing that for the Texas Cowboys, there would be no drinking while the young men were in uniform. It was a step in the right direction.

This alumni officer had graciously given me two tickets to the first home football game the following day against the University of Louisiana. It was the first game that the Cowboys were allowed back on the field. I had never been to a University of Texas football game or seen the Cowboys on the field or the cannon being shot when they scored a touchdown. I invited my girlfriend to go with me.

More than once I sat there with tears in my eyes in the hot Texas afternoon, the stadium full of cheering people, the cannon booming, exuding this huge cloud of smoke slowly drifting across the field onto our side of the stadium. I watched totally mesmerized with the 30 cheerleaders who, after every time UT scored, did back flips one by one as the crowd called out the score. I can still smell the smoke from the cannon and feel the excitement that filled that place.

The Cowboys were impressive to watch as they shot the cannon. Only six at a time were allowed onto the field, dressed in their full regalia of black levis, boots, long sleeved white shirts, burnt orange neckerchiefs, light brown chaps, and black felt creased cowboy hats.

It's no wonder Gabe wanted to belong to this group.

For a moment I reflected on all the events that had transpired since Gabe's death: his funeral, the investigation, the lawsuit. I reminisced that it had all been so hard to deal with and much harder to begin writing this book. I remembered reading Carl Branson's statement for the first time, dropping it and falling into a blue funk unable to go near my desk for three months.

Amidst the noise of the football game and the smell of the smoke from the cannon, there was another sweet fragrance in the air. It was the deep satisfaction that God had brought me through the grief and the anger. There were times it would surface, but not that day. Maybe the warm tingly feeling I felt all over was the hot September afternoon. Maybe it was Gabie showing me why he loved the University of Texas and the Cowboys so much and why he worked so hard to become one of them.

As I sat there, I also remembered that I had the choice to forgive or not to forgive this group. It was a hard thing to choose to forgive them. It had taken me the better part of those five years they were on probation to even come close to it.

Forgiveness is a choice. It's the choice between living in the bondage of bitterness or living in freedom. It is agreeing to live with the consequences of another person's sin. It's costly and we pay the price of the evil we forgive. We live with the consequences whether we want to or not.

God says He will "remember no more" our sins (Hebrews 10:17). Being omnipotent, God cannot forget, yet He loves us so much that He chooses to forgive and He chooses to forget. (When we ask Him to forgive us). He tosses it in the deep sea of forgetfulness.

In all honesty, I'll be first in line to admit that I used to fluctuate about the forgiveness thing. For years I had to continually work at it, wrestling through it. I found that forgiveness came easiest when I laid it down at Jesus' feet, realizing that I don't have all the answers. Only God knows everything that happened that night. I finally accepted that.

We were invited by the Texas Cowboy alum and his wife to the Texas Cowboys "shindig," which is Cowboy talk for the "after the game" party. Everyone was gracious and kind to us with that good ole Texan hospitality people in Texas are so famous for.

The entire room was full of excitement as the new Texas Cowboys, dressed in full regalia lined up before us as each one introduced themselves. I imagined what Gabe would have looked like and how proud he would have been to have been a Texas Cowboy.

As I stood there, it was as if I felt Gabe's presence. But he wasn't saying, "I'm OK, Mom. I'm OK," like he'd done five years earlier.

Instead, I was quietly whispering to him, "I'm OK now, Gabie. I'm OK."

~19~

THE HELMET AND THE PENNIES

Gabe's old Army helmet sits encased in the entrance to the Kappa Sig fraternity in Austin in memory of Gabe.

I still find pennies and other change, though I don't look for them anymore (and I have a ton of them). I used to think that maybe it was Gabe who put them down. But I truly believe that it's the angels who put the pennies down to bless us (regardless of who they use to do it).

If it's an important day, especially like a family reunion, I always find a penny or two just to remind me that Gabe's watching and that he is waiting for me and that I am loved and blessed.

I no longer hold my breath whenever I guzzle a whole glass of water. I used to do that many times every day as a reminder of what Gabe went through when he drowned. The deep wounds have finally healed.

Anyone who has lost a child knows that it's out of the order of things. No matter what age the child is or what age you are, losing a son or daughter is one of the worst experiences anyone can go through. Whatever the circumstances are, we need to remember that grieving is a natural process.

I was told to embrace grief and to fully experience it. The problem is that grief is one of the deepest negative emotions we can experience, and it can bring illness to the body. Though God has mercy on us and allows us to embrace grief for a time, lingering on it is not healthy.

At some point, we need to let it go.

It's like a butterfly that we set free.

Life is too short not to.

In Shakespeare's and Gabe's words:

"And this above all: to thine own self be true. And it must follow: as night the day, thou canst not then be false to any man. Farewell: my blessing season this in thee!"

To the Texas Cowboys, I'd like to say a few things.

I know it will sound like an oxymoron to say this after I've written this book, but I forgive you. I bless you. And I hope with everything in me that you will wear the right hat.

If ever there were a group of guys who deserve to wear the John Wayne hat and portray the John Wayne image, you do. You are a fantastic group of guys with a lot of potential. You have a huge community of people in Texas who love you and who will support you and see you through anything.

There's only one problem.

SECTION II

Hazing

~20~

HAZING DEFINED

Hazing is basically any wrongful act of initiation. If it's labeled an initiation, it very likely involves hazing.

The definition can get complicated. Hazing truly needs to be spelled out clearly because it is abuse and it can be misunderstood. Don't skip over reading this next part!

Hazing refers to any activity expected of someone joining a group (or maintaining status in a group) that humiliates, degrades or risks emotional and/or physical harm, regardless of the person's willingness to participate. In years past, hazing practices were typically considered harmless pranks or comical antics associated with young men in college fraternities. Today we know that hazing extends far beyond college fraternities and is experienced by boys/men and girls/women in school groups, university organizations, athletic teams, the military, and other social and professional organizations. Hazing is a complex social problem that is shaped by power dynamics operating in a group and/or organization and within a particular cultural context.

Hazing activities are *generally* considered to be: physically abusive, hazardous, and/or sexually violating. The specific behaviors or activities within these categories vary widely among participants, groups and settings. While alcohol use is common in many types of hazing, other examples of *typical* hazing practices include: personal servitude; sleep deprivation and restrictions on personal hygiene; yelling, swearing and insulting new members/ rookies; being forced to wear embarrassing or humiliating attire in public; consumption of bile substances or smearing of such on one's skin; brandings; physical beatings; binge drinking and drinking games; sexual simulation and sexual assault. [1]

Hank Nuwer adds to that: "Hazing is an activity that a high-status member orders other members to engage in or suggests that they engage in that in some way humbles a newcomer who lacks the power to resist, because he or she wants to gain admission to a group. Hazing can be noncriminal, but it is nearly always against the rules of an institution, team, or Greek group. It can be criminal, which means that a state statute has been violated. This usually occurs when a pledging-related activity results in gross physical injury or death." [2]

Senator Gonzalo Barrientos, D-Austin who wrote the Texas anti-hazing law in 1987, which made hazing a crime in Texas, defined hazing as "any intentional, knowing or reckless act, occurring on or off the campus of an educational institution … directed against a student, that endangers the mental or physical health or safety of a student for the purpose of pledging, or becoming a member of an organization." The law makes causing "serious bodily injury" during a hazing incident a felony under Texas state jurisdiction. [3]

Each state hazing law is different, though hazing is illegal in most states for good reason. It's been known to injure emotionally and physically, and occasionally leads to death. It happens not only on our college campuses, but has more recently spread to our high schools and even our junior highs, middle schools, and some grade schools in epidemic proportions.

Even though some of our state laws define what emotions or effects result from hazing, some of them don't specifically list hazing activities, possibly because hazing takes many forms. Hazing is an abuse that ranges from subtle to fatal. It can be verbal, physical, or mental and can be broken down into three distinct categories: subtle, harassment, and dangerous.

SUBTLE HAZING is often times harder to detect than physical hazing. These are actions against accepted standards of conduct and behavior, usually resulting in ridicule or humiliation.

> *Examples: lengthy telephone greetings, never doing anything with the pledge (or initiate), calling pledge "pledgie" or any other demeaning names, silence periods for pledges, any form of demerits, writing progress reports on pledges, requiring pledges to call members "Mr.", "Miss", etc, scavenger*

> hunts for meaningless objects, phone duty or house duties (if only assigned to pledges), requiring pledges to carry pledge handbook or paddles everywhere (to get signatures), scaring pledges with what may happen at initiation, deprivation of privileges.

Many think that these activities are harmless and constitute no danger to pledges. That may be the case, but stop and ask, what positive contributions do they bring? Are these activities benefiting or educating new pledges (or initiates)? Subtle hazing will also train the pledge to take on an attitude of servitude so that later when the activity of hazing worsens, the pledge is more open to allow it and participate in it because he has already regarded the act of hazing as a "harmless" activity and because this level of hazing seems to be "fun."

<u>HARRASSMENT HAZING</u> is found in activities that cause mental anguish, physical discomfort, confusion, frustration, or undue stress.

> Examples: sleep deprivation, verbal abuse, requiring pledges to answer questions under pressure, wearing ridiculous costumes or performing ridiculous activities, requiring only pledges to enter by the back door or go up back staircase, required to perform stunt or skit events that are demeaning or crude skits or poems, personal servitude such as carrying books, running errands, performing maid duties, performing lewd stunts, or restricting personal hygiene.

Many of the injuries, sometimes even deaths and lawsuits, have resulted from this level. While they seem harmless activities at the time, the problem is that they can get out of hand too quickly. One national fraternity was sued because a pledge deprived of sleep and under emotional duress, accidentally lost a testicle to a circular saw he was operating at the chapter house. The national fraternity was sued on the grounds that the pledge was impaired when he was forced to operate the power tool. The jury awarded the plaintiff $71,000. Many other injuries have been caused from raw eggs and other substances being dumped on or poured over pledges. Infections and hospital visits with IVs were the results.

<u>DANGEROUS OR VIOLENT HAZING</u> not only endangers the life of the initiate, but the lives of everyone else as well as the organization they represent. This includes any activity that has the potential to cause great physical harm or emotional damage.

Dangerous hazing can take the form of line-ups, kidnappings, forced drinking of alcohol, forced ingestion of vile substances, sexual violation, assault including branding or beating, burning, cattle prodding, paddlings, forced eating, restricting body movement (such as standing for long hours), intense calisthenics, dehydration, exposure to the weather, or the covering of bodies with foreign substances. [4]

RULE OF THUMB

- If you have to ask if it's hazing, it is.
- If in doubt, call your advisor/coach/national office. If you don't (call them), you already have your answer.
- If you haze, you have a low self-esteem.
- If you allow hazing to occur, you are a 'hazing enabler.'
- Failure to stop hazing has the potential to result in death. [5]

WHY JOIN A FRATERNITY KNOWING THEY HAZE?

Why do pledges allow themselves to be victimized?

1. PEER PRESSURE

A 1994 survey by the Phi Kappa Tau national fraternity found that peer pressure was the number one reason that pledges allowed themselves to be victimized. The study found that "pledges feel they have to prove themselves worthy to the actives so they will be accepted." They feel the need to "stick together" with their pledge class to get through the ordeal. For an incoming student, this is one of the most important aspects of college life, to be liked and accepted. They may feel that they need to "be tough," or "stick it out" etc, and prove their masculinity rather than risk being identified as a wimp or a sissy.

2. THE DESIRE TO BELONG

Another reason our young people will knowingly endure hazing is the desire to belong, which is a basic human need to have contact and reinforcement from others. As young people enter college, they search for independence and, at the same time, interdependence. As they detach from their parents and their home-life, they look for dependence upon their peers.

3. IT IS BLINDLY ACCEPTED

Hazing has permeated our culture, and it is blindly accepted. Hank

Nuwer believes that "Fraternity men honestly feel that they will lose quality young men if they don't continue the traditions. To them, hazing is fun and it is seen as part of a larger system because it is a part of American culture." Hazing practices can be seen in movies, businesses, athletics, and the military. The message – "If you want to be worthy of something great, then you are going to be challenged for it."

4. LACK OF EDUCATION

Many prospective members don't realize and are not informed about what the pledging process and hazing will entail because this information is shrouded in secrecy by the brotherhood or organization. Most pledges, or initiates, don't understand how bad it can get, how quickly it can get there or how to stop it. The increasing severity of hazing over the weeks and months of the pledging process places the pledge in a very vulnerable position, making him more susceptible to victimization.

5. GROUPTHINK MENTALITY

The term "Groupthink," penned by Irving Janis in 1972 in a book he authored called *Victims of Groupthink*, is defined as a mode of thinking that people engage in when joined together as a group. In this group atmosphere, sound, critical thinking deteriorates and members find justification in decision-making that they would normally consider wrong individually.

Janis wrote, "Groupthink is a mode of thinking that people engage in when they are deeply involved in a cohesive in-group ... members striving for unanimity override their motivation to realistically appraise alternative courses of action ... a deterioration of mental efficiency, reality, and moral judgment that results from group pressures.

"The group itself does not think of these things as impossible demands," he writes. "They themselves have gone through the initiation rite. The members merely tend to think of what they are doing as simply parallel to what they endured. It's a matter of misjudgment. None of them wants to commit manslaughter. It's a very sloppily made decision, one made in the stages of conviviality. Everyone perceives what is happening as in the range of what has always been done."

According to Janis, when pledges or brothers see their peers approving of something dangerous, silly, or inappropriate, *they are likely to join in* even if they would never have believed themselves capable of such acts. Janis states that the concept of peer pressure cannot be underestimated, citing studies that show people typically taking risks in a group setting that they would never take when alone. He adds that "the more amiability and esprit de corps among the members ... the greater the danger that independent critical thinking will be replaced by *group-think*." [6]

In the book: *When Will People Help in a Crisis?* John M. Darley wrote that it would be atypical for someone in a large group situation either to halt the aggressive behavior of another participant or to take positive action of any sort. It would seem that the more people who watch a victim in distress, the more chance there would be that someone would act to avert the tragedy. *But the opposite happens*! If each member of a fraternity is aware that other people are present, he will be *less* likely to act even if he thinks there is an emergency.

According to Hank Nuwer, author of four books on hazing, it is common for both hazers and pledges either to refuse to talk about hazing they have witnessed or to lie about it. The family and friends of hazing victims find it hard to accept that hazers feel that they face an impossible dilemma. By speaking the truth frankly, they break faith with a group that has tremendous importance to them at this stage of their lives. Whether it is a hockey player in a high-school hazing, a pledge or brother in a fraternity hazing, a neophyte about to enter some important adult secret society, or a serviceman in a military hazing, being a snitch or whistle-blower carries a terrible stigma in our society. At the same time, if hazers lie and say that hazing did not occur, they may still suffer tremendous guilt. Witnesses are in a no-win situation that must be recognized by anyone trying to interrogate them.

From the organization members' perspective, they want deserving people to join. The initiation becomes the litmus test for how much the students or pledges want to get in and how deserving they are.

From the students' standpoint, pledgeship and the initiation is a ritual for them, becoming a separation from where they were before to where they're going now. They value the organization, so they go through with it. They know members before have gone through it, so they want to go through it, too. [7]

"The hypothesis is 'I went through it, so you have to go through it' mentality. For guys, there's a bit of Machismo," says Dan Medlin, director of Greek affairs at the University of Texas. [8]

The group psychology is that students are following tradition and the tougher the initiation is, the more they'll value the group they're joining.

Despite stiff laws and more policing by colleges, hazing has an allure to some students, Hank Nuwer says. "It's attractive because it's forbidden. It points out the gap between people in authority and groups. People want to join groups and leave the establishment. It's attractive to be breaking the law to get into these groups," he says. [9]

Blane McCullough, an Austin psychotherapist who joined the Kappa Alpha fraternity at the University of Texas in 1982, says initiations create a special bond between members and pledges that isn't found in any other part of their life. "It's commonly known that people who are thrown together in great duress will form closer bonds than people who do not have to come together," he says. [10]

Yet when you combine peer pressure, secrecy, rebellion, and alcohol, you've got a tragedy waiting to happen.

FIVE COMMON MISCONCEPTIONS ABOUT HAZING

I. *"Hazing builds pledge class [or group] unity."* FACT: When hazing occurs, unity will be created within the pledge class, BUT the pledges will be unified *against* the fraternity chapter. The end result is a number of unified groups within one disunited chapter.

II. *"The pledges want to be hazed."* FACT: If you believe this, why not publicize your planned hazing activities during rush? Then see how many pledges the chapter gets.

III. *"I went through it; now the pledges have to go through it."* FACT: Would you go through it again? It only takes one class to break this so called "tradition." The founders and early members of most organizations and fraternities were not hazed, so why treat today's pledges differently?

IV. *"If we eliminate hazing, the fraternity will be just a social club instead of a fraternity. It will be a cakewalk to become a member."* FACT: A truly well organized, positive educational program will require more time, dedication, and energy than a hazing program. The resulting difference will be initiates who are better prepared to work for the chapter, and who can better serve as leaders.

V. *"The military thinks hazing is good, and they do it, so why can't we?"* FACT: The hazing in the military that is allowed is regimented and is done by professionals. It is done to prepare soldiers for their disciplined lifestyle. Military personnel are trained for unusual circumstances and to put their life on the line for our country. Fraternities don't ask that of their members. [11]

SO WHO IS RESPONSIBLE?

The answer? We are all responsible. This is not just a parent's problem, a teacher, coach, principal, school, fraternity or student's problem. To abolish hazing, it will take a combined force of students, alumni, universities, national levels of fraternity officers, and school administrations at middle school, junior high, high school and college levels.

If the American fraternity system is to be allowed in this century, changes must occur. The issue must be discussed and confronted, and a new understanding developed with better ways to educate. Ultimately the education of new members rests on the shoulders of *all* members, not just one officer or a single committee. It would greatly help if family members and friends understood the issue and stayed involved with their children.

When a student witnesses an act of hazing and does nothing, he condones the action and enables this disease of abuse and victimization to grow. He becomes just as guilty as the person who hazes. Any knowledge of hazing should be reported to the appropriate authorities. At the college level, it should be reported to the university dean of students, fraternity alumni, Greek advisor, the fraternity's National Administrative Office, and parents. At the high school and junior high level, the administration, school counselor, and parents should be notified.

To an outsider, hazing seems unbelievably absurd. But to a pledge—typically a freshman who has left home for the first time and wants desperately to fit in to this new kind of family, a brotherhood that promises a cliquish setting and masculine superiority, great parties and lots of available women—hazing is *not* punishment, it's a test of loyalty. It's a rite of passage into a world of male bonding, where his fraternity brothers will be friends for life.

"It's like child abuse. I'm not kidding," said Mark Buffkin, the president of the Pikes on the University of Texas campus. "You get hazed, so you want to haze. It's a vicious cycle that you just have to break." [12]

~21~

BULLYING

Bullying is not new. But it has recently become recognized as a serious social problem. A cousin to hazing, it has gone considerably out of control when we find incidents of kids killing other kids.

Hazing in our high schools and universities might not be such an enigma if the bullying problems in our grade schools, middle schools, junior highs, and high schools were not such a problem. In fact, areas of the country where there are policies of zero tolerance toward bullying in the schools generally have fewer hazing incidents, particularly effecting the college level.

It was later discovered that the two young men who committed the Columbine High School murders in Littleton, Colorado (1999) "had been routinely shoved in lockers and ridiculed," thrown into their lockers *daily*. They went to the high school's counselors and administration many times complaining of the problem. The school did nothing. [1]

When a child is bullied, regardless of his or her age, he has almost no legal retaliation without the help of an adult. If the administration doesn't step in and defend the victim, the child can quite easily develop symptoms of uncontrollable anger and social behavior, contributing to teenage suicide or worse.

The definition of bullying involves any harassment, intimidation, act or threat that would harm the student, damage a student's property, place a student in reasonable fear of harm to his or her person, place a student in fear or damage to his or her property, OR, where the victim is being treated severely and persistently, that it creates an intimidating, threatening, or abusive educational environment for the student.

In order to understand how to deal with the act of a child being bullied, we must understand and define the characteristics of a bully:

The definitions of a *School Bully* involve the following:

1. Refusal (not inability) to think rationally about himself/herself and others,
2. Small scale terrorist, with behavior, mostly taking place during school time,
3. Justifies terrorist activities towards others with self psychological excuses ("I want to appear to be in control"),
4. Enjoys enforcing power on others and causing extreme fear
5. Over-bearing person who tyrannizes the weak
6. To rule by intimidation and terror
7. Threatening or acts of violence on others. [2]

The only difference between a terrorist and a bully is in the organized planning or cause of the activity and the scale of terror. A bullied child will believe that there is no difference between a terrorist and a bully, given the above definitions.

Ninety percent of students feel being bullied causes social, emotional, or academic problems. Studies show that both bullies and victims have problems later in life because of bullying.

Sixty-nine percent of students believe schools respond poorly to reports of bullying. Three out of four students report that they have been bullied. Each month over 250,000 students report being physically attacked.

For school safety and to protect our children, a new organization has evolved, called "Bully Police, USA." They are found at: www.bullypolice.org. There are other groups surfacing to do the same thing, such as "WeTip," which can be found at www.wetip.com, or you can call 1-800-78-CRIME(27463). They are encouraging states, school systems, and administrations to implement laws and actions to protect our children against school bullies. They also encourage counseling for both groups (bullies and victims) to overcome this.

If you or your children experience any problems with bullying after going to the school administration and asking them to help you, log onto either or both these websites, get educated, and inform your school about this.

There IS something you can do to stop bullying!

~22~

BINGE DRINKING

One Friday night three weeks after school started in the fall of 1997, John Eric Stinner (rhymes with winner), a freshman at Frostburg State University in Frostburg, Maryland, decided to go to a non-sanctioned fraternity party. He had called his mother the day before and asked her if she could drive over to pick him up Friday night. She told him she couldn't because the weather over the pass was too bad to drive. She asked him to take the bus Saturday morning and she would meet him halfway.

That night John went with a friend to a Kappa Beta Zeta fraternity party where he drank at least 12 shots of hard liquor plus eight beers in a period of two hours. He passed out and was taken to his dorm room "to sleep it off."

John died in his sleep two hours later at 11:00 p.m. His body was not discovered until the next evening (Saturday) when his roommate, a football player who had played a game out of town, came home late. John's blood alcohol content was 0.34. His death was never cited as hazing, but should have been.

Eight students at Frostburg State University were charged with manslaughter; seven were convicted. Judge J. Frederick Sharer gave each of the defendants a 90-day suspended jail sentence and placed them on five years of probation. They were also each fined $1,000 and ordered to perform 250 hours of community service, citing that "They did act without care or concern for others in their rush to have a good time." Diane

Stinner still grieves that she didn't drive over the pass and pick her son up for the weekend. [1]

Four months later, statistics showed that John's death hadn't slowed down the drinking problem in Frostburg. Loud parties continued with drunkenness, fights and public urinations, stemming from drinking parties. [2]

Binge drinking can involve as many as five drinks in one hour for females, seven in one hour for males. Some binges of drinking last three or four days over a period of many weeks. Some binges are only once a week. This is not social drinking involving two to four drinks over a period of five hours. This involves a lot of alcohol intake over a short period of time.

One doesn't last long in college at that rate. Many flunk out from their inability to control it. The fraternity lifestyle of partying "till you drop" many times involves competition drinking with shots of hard liquor (which is likely what John Stinner did).

The most dangerous hazing involves alcohol poisoning and contributes to 80% of deaths due to hazing. It's estimated that hundreds of deaths due to alcohol have occurred each year in our colleges, most of them unreported. These incidents have likely involved drinking contests, forced drinking, or using various alcoholic mixtures to induce vomiting.

Varying degrees of tolerance are caused by an individual's inability to filter out the "poisons," the effect of sugars, possible allergies, medications still in the bloodstream, the number of drinks ingested and how quickly they are taken, the alcohol content or potency, the person's activities while drinking, how much food is ingested before or during drinking, and body weight.

When a person begins to black out, it is a sign of the assault on all body organs and must never be dismissed as "nothing is wrong," or he "can just sleep it off." The problem for the onlooker is distinguishing the difference. One sign to look for is if too much alcohol has been ingested too quickly, especially if the person is not used to drinking.

The progression, if not stopped, is that one-by-one, the internal organs go into a state of shock and become numb until they are non-functional. The heart is generally the last organ to be affected. Breathing becomes labored and in the last stages, the body will turn cold and purple or blue from lack of oxygen. The heart eventually slows down and quits beating.

A person in this condition can be taken to the emergency room, but it's not an absolute that they will live. All the hospital can do is pump their stomach and put them on an IV and oxygen. Sometimes they can be revived, sometimes not.

After drinking, many victims are set aside to "sleep it off," and either drown in their own vomit or die of intoxication. (One should never lay a person on his back to sleep it off.)

Most states consider "legally drunk" to be a blood alcohol level of 0.08. Authorities believe that a person with that level of intoxication is unable to drive a car primarily because the perception and reaction times are too slow. Higher degrees of intoxication, such as 0.20 and 0.30 endanger the victim all the more. Drunkenness certainly jeopardizes all involved if allowed behind the wheel of a vehicle.

When a person's alcohol level reaches 0.40 or higher, it is so severe that very few recover without immediate help. Many deaths have occurred among young college age people due to overdoses of alcohol, some with an intoxication level as low as 0.26.

Teenage drinking is a problem that can't be overlooked. Many young people think they are experienced and aren't. They see everyone else doing it, so it must be OK to indulge, not fully understanding the negative effects alcohol can have on the body. Alcohol is too easily available and is an acceptable indulgence, whether the reason is to kill the pain, peer pressure, or just to "party." One mistake can too quickly take a life, whether it's your own or someone else's.

Most young people are not educated enough about the dangers of alcohol. College represents a time of being out of the home for the first time. The real danger comes when peer pressure and the simple desire to belong and to be accepted are in the mix. Add hazing and you've got a dangerous recipe for disaster.

From a parent's point of view, it's a grievous thing that something so precious to us as our child's life can be put so quickly in danger without any warning. Receiving the phone call of your child's death is not something you are ever prepared for. One of the best defenses is having a healthy relationship with your child.

Yet, that's what Dianne Stinner said she had with her son John.

~23~

HAZING STORIES

HAZING ISN'T JUST "GOOD CLEAN FUN!"

"Justice is turned back and righteousness stands afar off; for truth is fallen in the street and equity cannot enter. So truth fails… Then the Lord saw it, and it displeased Him that there was no justice."

– Isaiah 59:14, 15

HIGHLAND HIGH SCHOOL HAZING

In July 2002, a high school initiation took place here in my hometown of Pocatello, Idaho. More than once I heard from the seniors and their parents that this private party was "just good, clean fun," and that the school system ought to "butt out." It appalled me.

I had been asked to be on the DDRC (District Disciplinary Review Committee) whose objective was to assess the situation and decide the appropriate punishment on behalf of the school system regarding the ten students the police had ticketed. As each of those students came before the board, I kept hearing denial of any hazing activities. Because it had taken place during the summer at a private residence involving kids from many organizations, the parents and upper classmen claimed that it didn't have anything to do with school. Yet this coed hazing did involve a specific group: the popular kids, the "in" group.

As students appeared before the committee, I asked three of them to define hazing. They all three believed that hazing was something that happened in college that involved drinking and paddling.

The July initiation/private party was attended by ninety high school kids, thirty-three of them initiates (all ninth and tenth grade students because Pocatello just moved ninth grade freshmen into the high schools). It involved a great deal of hazing.

For the fifteen boys, it involved putting "blue ice" on their privates; later they were given two eggs to put into their shorts and they were told to hump each other until the eggs broke; 14 dozen eggs were pelted against them. The 9th graders were allowed to leave and the 10th graders had to roll around on a tarp laden with ketchup, cat food, dirt, water and female douche (which got into their eyes).

The eighteen girls were required to wear their clothes inside out and backwards with their undies on top. The two girls who were on their period were excused from wearing their panties and top and told to tie tampons to dangle from their fingers (not enforced), some girls were "patted" on the butt by seniors; they had to wash their makeup off with water from the hose and a bar of soap, their hair was shampooed with a conglomeration of ketchup and syrup, they were told to put marshmallows in their armpits and run across the yard in front of the boys four times in wet T-shirts, then they had to eat the marshmallows. One girl had a heart problem and after doing all the above became tired and was sent home. The remaining girls had to dance on the balcony steps before the crowd of 60, mostly boys who hooted, hollered, and wolf whistled.

Neighbors said they watched some of it and thought it was a perfectly acceptable private party and argued about it being "hazing."

The punishment involved community work for everyone who was there; several were put on probation and/or suspended from government classes (these kids were the leaders of the school), football games and cheerleading. No one was suspended. I personally think the penalties weren't severe enough: the handful of kids who planned this should have received much steeper penalties and at least two or three of them should have been suspended.

The video that was taken of all this was never confiscated. It should have been subpoenaed by the school district. Most of the kids had to go to one of two classes that were supposed to teach about hazing. In my estimation the subject of hazing was not taught correctly or complete enough. The school system's insurance salesman taught it! I was asked only to share about what happened to Gabe. Parents became verbally abusive at the end of the meetings, and the accused high school kids still didn't "get it" about hazing because it was never properly explained. Their entire premise was that it was a harmless party. Harmless to who? If anything involves hazing, like this party definitely did, it can psychologically injure young people, plus if anything had gone wrong, like it oftentimes does, someone could have been injured. Oddly enough, the school usually gets blamed.

During the DDRC meetings, three of the accused hired the same lawyer who contested my presence on the board because I knew about and had experienced "hazing." The book of regulations clearly states that no one can be on the board with any knowledge of the particular wrong doing, so the accusation was completely unfounded.

The good news is that the following year, the student government at Highland High School instigated a zero tolerance for hazing and it completely changed the school's attitude toward hazing, also influencing the other two high schools in town. Things like the baseball team in another high school elected to have their new guys take them out to dinner instead of hazing them.

GLENBROOK NORTH HIGH SCHOOL, CHICAGO

On May 4th, 2003, in the upscale Chicago suburb of Northbrook Village, high school sophomore girls paid $25 for the opportunity to go through an initiation called "powder puff." Six of the twenty initiates were later taken to the hospital, one with a broken leg, another requiring several stitches for a gash on the crown of her head from a thrown bottle, and another for a concussion from being hit in the head with a baseball bat (she was wearing a bucket on her head). Poured over them were buckets of paint, mud, human feces, chicken entrails, and garbage, some of it mashed into their faces.

A 1996 graduate of the high school stated she felt that the crime should have been seen as an "attempted murder" and prosecuted as such.

Two young men videotaped the event. Weeks later, the *Oprah Winfrey Show*, based out of Chicago, aired the videotapes on national TV. Oprah read a statement from one of the young men: "I saw it happening and I did nothing. I made the conscious decision to attend the event, knowing to a certain extent what was about to unfold. We had no comprehension of the degree that this event would escalate. It got out of hand so fast that I lost sight of what was actually occurring around me. I lost focus of my position, my role in this situation and my capability to intervene. I fell into the mob mentality. I subjected myself to the level of people I've never respected in my life. And I lost respect for myself."

Fifteen teenagers were charged with misdemeanor battery: a dozen girls and three boys. Thirty-one, all but three of them girls, were given ten-day suspensions from school. Two adults were charged, one with purchasing alcohol and the other with allowing underage drinking in their home. Another teenager was charged for transporting the alcohol. All present who were responsible for the hazing were suspended from the senior prom and other extracurricular activities, plus they were barred from their graduation ceremony.

Parents of those seniors scheduled a separate graduation and senior prom. Attorneys for the students said the incident had received a lot more attention than it deserved.

At the end of the *Oprah Winfrey Show*, one lady commented: "I don't like casting a dark shadow over an area of our community, but I do feel good about the kind of debate that's being created ... also about the parental discussions. Hopefully, there will be a student next time who will stand up and do something about it." [*Before* it gets out of hand!] [1]

"Hazing has escalated to behavior that is now horrible, shocking and producing many injuries," says Norman Pollard, director of the counseling center at New York's Alfred University, who coauthored a 2000 study that showed nearly half of U.S. high school students experienced some form of hazing rituals, ranging from silly to lethal. [1]

JIM KNOLL, UNIVERSITY OF NEBRASKA

One Friday afternoon in the spring of 1993, freshman Jim Knoll finished his last class for the week and started walking down the hallway at the University of Nebraska, wondering what he was going to do that weekend. He thought he'd just go back to his dorm room and then over to the Sigma Nu fraternity where he had just begun pledging a month earlier.

In the hallway he was kidnapped and blindfolded by three guys who led him across campus to the Sigma Nu fraternity house where he was taken up to the third floor, handcuffed to a wooden chair, and locked in a small bathroom.

They took his blindfold off and told him that he had been accepted as an active into the fraternity. He was told that each of the 50 or more actives would be coming into the bathroom to congratulate him, each with a shot of hard liquor as a sign of acceptance into the fraternity.

Jim lost count after twelve or thirteen visits and had no idea how much liquor he ingested, he guessed it was somewhere around 20 shots. When the visits slowed down, he busted the wooden chair to free himself, climbed up onto the sink, opened the window above the sink and crawled out, shimmying down a drainpipe.

Jim would have gotten successfully down had the drainpipe not broken. They figure he fell two or three stories directly onto his face landing on the hard pavement below. No one knows for sure how far he fell. He was so drunk he doesn't remember. The fall shattered every bone in his face.

Jim's blood alcohol level was 0.45, over four times the state's legal drinking limit and high enough to be a death sentence. The hospital immediately pumped his stomach and put him on oxygen and an IV. They prayed. Had he remained in the bathroom, he most assuredly would have passed out and died of alcohol poisoning.

I met Jim and his dad on the *Maury Povich Show* in the fall of 1998. He was lucky to be alive and looked in good health. He had survived five reconstructive surgeries on his face and was told that he would probably never be able to taste or smell anything again. He lost his sight for a few days and his hearing for several weeks, which is still bad. His cognitive abilities were impaired and the prognosis was that he would probably never be able to finish college.

Though Jim is a nice looking young man whose face looks perfectly normal, his life was drastically changed by the irresponsible actions of this fraternity.

His parents sued the National Sigma Nu fraternity for six million dollars. [2]

WILLIAM (TREY) WALKER III, TEXAS A & M

Late one night on an unusually cold evening January 8th, 1997, at Texas A & M at Bryan/College Station, the pledges of the Phi Gamma Delta, nicknamed FIJIs, were told to strip down to their underwear.

Earlier that day they had been required to strip wallpaper, clean, sand, and paint the upstairs of the fraternity house. During a brief break, one of the pledges had spit into an active's beer. The active found out later, and to punish the pledges, they were told to strip down to their shorts in the freezing January night and were hosed down outside (it was 33 degrees during an ice storm). Still wet and very cold, the pledges were locked in the garage.

Eighteen year old Trey, an otherwise large, healthy athlete, was an asthmatic who never went anywhere without his inhaler. The actives had taken his inhaler earlier that day. In the garage he lapsed into a serious asthmatic attack. The pledges were unable to do anything for him. Several actives had intermittently told the president of the Fiji's many times through the day and evening that Trey was having problems breathing, but he would not be bothered.

By the time the actives opened the garage door Trey was no longer breathing. The fraternity members later claimed that they allowed Trey to use his inhaler, but it did not work. Instead of taking him immediately to the hospital a four-minute drive away, they chose to leave his purple body in a coma in the next room while they busied themselves contriving a story to cover up their lack of judgment.

The doctor at the hospital emergency room later told Trey's parents that if the fraternity members had taken him straight to the emergency room even after he had collapsed and quit breathing, he probably could have been revived. By the time the police got there, he was dead.

The Fijis were originally suspended for three years. The fraternity changed their story twice before the truth came out during the trial. After convincing the authorities that his death had nothing to do with hazing, they successfully got the suspension retracted to two years.

When I was in Texas in 1997, I met Trey's parents, who were still going through much grief and a grueling court battle.

Robin Walker, a successful watercolor artist has since written a book about her stepson's death. [3]

EILEEN STEVENS AND C.H.U.C.K.

One bitterly cold evening in February 24, 1978, when the temperature was nine degrees Fahrenheit in upstate New York at Alfred University, Chuck Stenzel was kidnapped from his dorm, locked in the trunk of a car and given a pint of bourbon, a fifth of wine, and a six-pack of beer and told to consume it before he was released. Forty minutes later when they opened the trunk, he was unconscious. They put him to bed at the Klan Alpine fraternity house where everyone assumed he would "sleep it off."

He didn't. Chuck died that night of acute alcohol poisoning.

"Your son didn't have a chance," the pathologist said, "and I can tell you one other thing. I'm sure that it was not your son's experience with alcohol that killed him. It was his lack of experience. His body went into shock and his heart stopped. I can't believe he was left to sleep it off."

It was not until after his funeral that they found out that he had gone to a fraternity party that night.

In August of 1978, Mrs. Stevens launched a national fight against hazing. With the help of her sister, she formed C.H.U.C.K., an acronym for the Committee to Halt Useless College Killings.

The Stevens' filed a civil suit against Alfred University, Klan Alpine, and its officers in August 1978. The school consistently denied responsibility for Chuck's death, claiming the incident occurred off campus at a private fraternity party. Four years after Chuck died, the lawsuit was resolved in the Stevens' favor by an out-of-court settlement with the fraternity and one of its officers. Alfred University was dropped from the lawsuit.

Mrs. Stevens' story has been told in magazines all over the country. A book was written and a movie was made of this, both called *Broken Pledges*. She has been on *Phil Donahue, Oprah Winfrey, 20/20, Today, Good Morning America, Tomorrow, Hour Magazine*, and hundreds of radio and television programs. She has traveled extensively, sharing her story and her information on hazing with state legislatures, national Greek conferences, universities, media, local civic groups, and individual and national fraternity groups. Eileen Stevens has been pivotal in instigating and encouraging each state to implement laws against hazing. [4]

HAZING IN GENERAL

The following is an excerpt from one of Eileen's speeches and uniquely describes hazing:

So often, the details of hazing are hidden in secrecy. Or the death by hazing is listed as an accident. Injuries and abuses often go unreported.

By far, acute intoxication is the leading cause of death in fraternity hazing incidents. Alcohol is somehow related to ninety-seven per cent of all hazing deaths. The next most common cause of death in fraternity hazing activities are from the accidents that occur during "road trips" or "kidnappings." Following that, other statistics are from "exercise sessions" or "workout nights."

One pledge choked to death on his vomit after being made to run until he was exhausted; another choked to death trying to swallow a thick slice of oil-coated liver. One boy suffocated when the "grave" he had been forced to dig and lie in collapsed on top of him. Another fell to his death from a coffin suspended by chains above a gorge.

Pledges participating in "exercise nights" have died of stroke or heat exhaustion. Some of these men have had medical problems that they did not know about or were too embarrassed about to reveal to their friends. A number of pledges have drowned after being thrown into rivers, lakes, or creeks. Pneumonia has killed other pledges from being hazed outside in extreme temperatures.

One boy died of a skull fracture after being told to jump, blindfolded, into a water tank, which nobody realized was empty. Pledges who have been taken away from campus and left lost or intoxicated to find their way back home have been hit and killed by cars, fallen to their deaths from high ledges, shot as trespassers, thrown from moving vehicles, gored by a bull, or found beaten and in a coma by the side of the road. Others have been branded with coat hangars, cattle brands, or dry ice. [5]

MENTAL HAZING

Examples of "mental hazing" or mind games, thought by many hazers to be harmless because they don't inflict any stress physically include sleep deprivation, lineups in which pledges are falsely told they have been black-balled while others were accepted as members, interrogation sessions in which pledges are made to reveal their sexual histories and other intimacies, lying to pledges to humiliate or confuse them, isolation tactics, ostracization, and labeling pledges with demeaning personal knicknames.

According to the Chicago Tribune, blindfolded pledges at Miami University of Ohio had to volunteer a testicle while a whirring chainsaw was held close to their bodies to intimidate them. Syracuse University pledges traveled their campus with dead fish tied around their necks. Other Syracuse pledges leaped onto a four-inch "nail" sticking out of a board. The nail turned out to be aluminum foil. The Klan Alpine fraternity had pledges jump into a pile of "broken glass," which was really only corn flakes.

The earliest recorded methods of mental hazing occurred at Brown University in 1922, replacing the "time-honored custom of paddling" by substituting mental torture from methods learned in psychology courses. The front page of the New York *Times* article stated: "Two of the leading fraternities have adopted the new system and are pronouncing their work good. Others are expected to follow, as the results are declared to leave the initiated in a much more tractable state of mind and imbued with a 'proper sense of his unworthiness.'"

In her experiences Eileen Stevens found that the more she learned about hazing, the more disturbed she became about the fraternity system's downplaying of mind games. The pledges who had experienced mind games would share their experiences with her, some crying uncontrollably when they talked about their ordeals, then afterwards experiencing shame and anger. One frequent caller stuttered; another harbored *killing* anger. *Only mental indeed*, she thought.

ALL HAZING IS WRONG

At first Eileen fought only against dangerous hazing practices. But she grew more intolerant of all hazing, after coming to the conclusion that many fatalities and injuries are the consequence of activities that start as so-called good, clean fun. To ask hazers to draw their own lines was foolish and unrealistic. She came to see that all hazing was inherently wrong. No rationalization can justify it.

After her appearance on *Donahue* in the late 70's, she received letters like the one from a Texas man who wrote her to say that hazing, when controlled, established bonds. The basic attitude was that someone else's hazing was horrible, but you just can't know the extenuating circumstances behind our hazing, lady. "I feel our fraternity was an exception to the rule," said the letter writer. "We were not forced to drink except once – a hot Jax with a raw egg in it, and the most of what happened was someone threw up."

On a substance abuse panel, Eileen was confronted by a male student who related: "[Hazing] made me a better person," he said. "I don't perceive hazing as something negative." Eileen responded: "I'm not liking what you're saying, but I think you're speaking for a lot of people," she said. "You are courageous enough to speak what other people are feeling. Yet if your best friend were injured, or if you were, maybe you'd feel differently."

Eileen learned that the foolish and dangerous practice of hazing was more complicated than she had at first suspected. She began to hope that once hazers and the hazed came to understand their behavior, they might adopt safe, undemeaning alternatives.

She heard the same tune and similar lyrics: Don't highlight our bad side, the Greeks said: highlight our good side. But she believed that the dark side must be illuminated before it can be eliminated.

As much as she would come to appreciate what was good and decent about fraternities, the vision of her son Chuck's death kept her from making compromises that violated her organization's founding principles. Hazing has been, for Eileen, a mad troll the Greeks keep chained in their collective attics; she wanted the beast tamed. There could be no compromise in her mind. [6]

Upon reading about Eileen Steven's story I came to a deeper understanding and appreciation of the problems with fraternities and the whole Greek system. I agree with her that once we understand how huge the problem is, maybe we can become less against the Greeks and more adamantly against hazing and the issues that revolve around it.

For more hazing stories, go to www.stophazing.com.

~24~

PROBLEMS AT UNIVERSITY OF TEXAS

"Maybe there are other universities with worse fraternity systems, but I'm not aware of them," said Eileen Stevens, who started the organization, C.H.U.C.K. (Committee to Halt Useless College Killings). "I'm sorry, but the University of Texas comes up time and again as a blatant, arrogant system," she said in an interview for Texas Monthly magazine. [1]

Problems associated with this type of gang behavior are particularly acute at the University of Texas. Hank Nuwer, author of *Broken Pledges, The Deadly Rite of Hazing*, a nationally recognized expert on hazing, said UT is regarded as one of the worst universities in the country for hazing. [2]

When the University of Texas' own staff advisor to the fraternities and sororities, Sherri Sanders, went to national Greek conferences for advisors (years ago), she said "they always ask me about the 'Texas mentality' among the fraternities. They think fraternities here are so macho that they are practically impossible to control." [3]

The 1987 University of Texas task force studying fraternity problems discovered that national fraternal officers referred to the "Texas Mentality," a mentality defined in the report – recognized as one of the best available – as a tolerance for hazing and excessive alcohol consumption.

The 1989 Texas anti-hazing law didn't seem to have slowed the fraternities down. Soon after the law was passed, a black Austin bus driver reported to the police that at least fifty SAEs (Sigma Alpha Epsilon) had surrounded him and shouted racial insults. A mother anonymously reported that, as part of a Phi Delta Theta (Phi Delt) fraternity ritual, her son and other pledges were taken to a "retreat," where they were beaten and shot with shotgun pellets from a distance.

Although the University of Texas fraternities are chapters of well-known national fraternal organizations, within the UT frat world itself there is a distinct and sometimes harsh caste system. At the bottom are small fraternities, each with about twenty to sixty members thought of by some as the "geeks of the Greeks," including black fraternities, an Asian American and a Hispanic fraternity. The middle group consists of fraternities with 70 to 120 members. At the top of the UT frat world is the elite group, known as the Big Six – the KAs (Kappa Alphas), the SAEs (Sigma Alpha Epsilon), the Pikes (Pi Kappa Sigma), the Sigma Phi's (Sigma Phi Epsilons), the Delts (Delta Tau Deltas) and the Fijis (Phi Gamma Deltas). They are the classic, old money fraternities, with approximately 140 members or more and annual budgets that go over $1,000,000 [this figure is probably considerably higher now]. These are the guys who, in high school, were football stars or the most-popular figures among the in-group and have always been considered prize dates for the UT sororities. "You're told early that those six are the cool ones to be with," a member of a prominent sorority said. "If you go out with an SAE, it's considered pretty cool, not because of who he is, but because he's an SAE."

Their lofty positions in Greek circles were one of the advantages of growing up wealthy. Although a few of them grew up among notable small-town families, the majority were raised in the bigger Texas cities, many graduating from prominent high schools. Most of their fathers are bankers, lawyers, oilmen, or politicians, filling positions of trust and power within the Texas establishment. These young men are very aware of who one another's fathers are and how much they are worth. For them, the lesson is learned early: To make it as a man around here, one has to make money. Most of the talk around these fraternities involves status and influence.

"Because the alums are so powerful, Fijis have always considered themselves untouchable, a little better than the rest of us," one rival frat president said. One method of establishing the status of acceptance into a fraternity during rush is to gain access to tax information (finding out how much money Daddy makes), a formula also observed by the sororities at UT.[4]

The Greeks are considered bedfellows with the University of Texas because of the close alliance of academia with the Greeks' social world, so UT has to walk a tight-rope keeping them in line.

Several years ago, two of the Big Six were abruptly shut down: the Pikes (Pi Kappa Alpha) in 1997, and the Kappa Alphas (KAs) in 2001.

For a time, the Big Six became the Big Four.

PI KAPPA ALPHA

On the weekend of October 11-13, 1996, the 170-member Pi Kappa Alpha fraternity at University of Texas hazed their pledges in an initiation that brought eleven violations against them the next spring. The UT officials found that the pledges were made to stand at attention for hours, the first portion of it with their hands behind their heads. They were shocked with cattle prods, forced to eat things containing high quantities of cayenne and smokeless tobacco, burned with cigarettes and cigars on their backs, shoulders and arms, smeared food over them, required to bend over and be paddled, told to perform calisthenics in their underwear, required to purchase and drink alcohol, wear embarrassing or uncomfortable clothing, lined up and demeaned, asked embarrassing questions, yelled at, pushed, pelted with substances like syrup and flour, and then told not to cooperate with the university's investigation.

That fall during the initiation, while standing at attention for hours, one pledge began to faint, catching himself with his foot. An active quickly reacted and broke a couple of the pledge's toes with a hammer.

That pledge went to the police and reported the incident.

After it was investigated, the pledge returned to get his clothes and was threatened with a baseball bat. Fearing for his life, the pledge dropped out of school and moved to another university out of state to finish college.

The University learned about the hazing through anonymous phone calls. The allegations were originally denied by both the actives and the pledges.

The assault charge against the active who broke the pledge's toes was considered a Class A misdemeanor and was punishable by up to a year in jail and a fine up to $4,000. A terroristic threat charge against another pledge and the hazing charges against the others were Class B misdemeanors punishable by up to three months in jail and a $2,000 fine. One hundred and twenty-one members of the Pikes were kicked out of the fraternity for hazing allegations. Hazing charges were issued against nine members of Pi Kappa Alpha and the fraternity was banned for three years.

The fraternity tried to cover up the hazing by encouraging the pledges not to cooperate with the University's investigation. At first, they did not cooperate with the University. Information was only forthcoming when the pledges were questioned a second time. [5]

SIGMA NU

Years earlier in November 1990, another incident took place that shut down another of the "big six." After a Sigma Nu pledge was beaten and led around the room with a claw hammer gripping his testicles, the Sigma Nu fraternity was banned for three years.

A few alumni happened to be visiting the Sigma Nu fraternity. About two in the morning, they called one of the pledges: a junior premed student from Fort Worth living in Austin, and told him to come over. After he and at least three other pledges arrived, according to court affidavits, the actives and alumni hit him twenty times with a paddle and then took him to the Pit, a small room behind the stairs with a dirt floor, where he was forced to do push-ups after disrobing. They pushed his face into the dirt floor while someone walked on his back. They poked him eight times in the stomach with a broom handle. They used the claw end of a hammer to lead him around by the testicles. They ordered him to run around the fraternity house while holding a large rock over his head. Then, using lighter fluid, someone set the crotch of his blue jeans on fire.

The next morning the student's mother received an anonymous phone call telling her that her son was "in trouble." She immediately left Ft. Worth arriving at the Sigma Nu house in Austin four hours later, going directly to his room. He wasn't there. She called his name to no avail. She wandered down the hall and asked several guys if they'd seen him. No one knew where he was. She went back to the room, sat on his bed to contemplate the situation and heard a whimper coming from the large walk-in closet. Opening the closet doors, she found her big, burly son cowering in the back corner of the closet.

His head looked up and caught her eyes. He was in serious pain, emotionally and physically. He slowly got up and joined her in the room. As she stood there dumbfounded, he painfully whispered, "Mom, you won't believe what they did to me."

He was referring to his buttocks and thighs, black and blue with bruises, his privates burning, reddened from the fire. The traumatized young man continued in a hushed voice, "Don't let any of the others know where I am. They'll come kill me."

She was shocked. "Get your things. We're leaving."

After returning to Ft. Worth, his mother reported the incident to officials from the Sigma Nu national office who quickly arrived in Austin, conducted a brief investigation, then revoked the charter of the UT chapter. The seven students involved in the hazing were either put on probation or expelled by UT. [6]

HISTORY OF FRATERNITIES AT UNIVERSITY OF TEXAS/ AUSTIN

In the 1900's the *Daily Texan* was already after UT's fraternities, labeling them "pretty little boys," and in 1913 more than 600 non-frat students met to demand the ouster of all fraternities due to their exclusivity.

Fraternities, which began cropping up in American universities during the 1820's, were never created out of some pure desire for brotherly love. Wealthy, ambitious, socially oriented college men, then the biggest rebels on campus, needed a refuge from college faculties and administrators who thought college should be a period of self-abnegation, prayer, and study. To avoid prying eyes, these men created Greek-letter organizations, pledged themselves to secrecy, adopted some Masonic ritual techniques for their initiation ceremonies, and started living the good life.

In Texas, bills to abolish fraternities were presented in the Legislature in 1913, 1915, 1925, and 1929, but they all failed. In 1928, during a Delta Kappa Epsilon initiation a football player named Nolte McElroy fainted and died after being forced to wear wet pajamas and crawl through two bedsprings that had been charged with electricity. University of Texas, embarrassed by the incident, ruled the death an accident, encouraging the fraternities to promise to eliminate "horseplay" from their initiations.

By 1929, Greeks dominated UT life. Back then hazing was an accepted part of fraternity life. Verbal abuse and humiliating physical acts were methods used to temporarily strip away a pledge's individual dignity in order to find dignity in the group. As a result, on winter evenings, pledges would be taken on "rides" out of town, where they would be left naked to find their own way home. They would wear burlap shirts with strings of garlic around their necks to class. They had to participate in such games as the Barn Dance, in which they would crawl naked around the floor while actives shot raw lima beans from a slingshot at their bottoms. "I suppose we never got in trouble for any of it because no one was hurt or killed," said noted movie producer and writer William D. Wittliff, a UT Kappa Sigma in the late fifties, who, like other older frat men, sheepishly recalls his hazing days only after great coaxing.

Fraternities remained strong until the late sixties when anti-war demonstrations hit UT and social events were considered frivolous. By 1976 the fraternity antics were back. Phi Delt pledges, covered with molasses and cornflakes were found by the police in the back of a U-Haul truck. The Kappa Sigs were caught forcing their pledges to eat a concoction of raw eggs, jalapenos, Limburger cheese and cod-liver oil. The Texas Cowboys were caught using cattle prods on initiates [picture enclosed]. Even the Longhorn band was suspended after burning several freshmen with dry ice in a mock-branding exercise.

The 1978 release of *Animal House*, the sex-crazed, car-crashing fraternity movie, didn't help matters. In the 70s the Phi Delts at UT were attending a mixer with a sorority, but the young women, disgusted with the fraternity men's "smart-ass attitude," left the party early. The next day, the Phi Delts sent a box of doughnuts over to the sorority house as a way of apologizing. A few hours later, they sent over photographs of what they had done with those doughnuts before sending them: Their penises were sticking through the doughnut holes.

By the mid-eighties, fraternity life was out of control. The Alpha Tau Omega fraternity, once one of the most distinguished Greek groups on campus, was disbanded by its national organization after a pledge underwent surgery for an infection as a result of being locked in a room with twenty other pledges for 72 hours and pelted with raw eggs.

In 1986, in a booze-sodden initiation rite, Phi Kappa Psi brothers handcuffed eighteen-year-old Mark Seeburger to the inside of a van and had him drink 16 to 20 ounces of rum (roughly twenty highballs) in less than two hours while they drove around. He was then dragged to his dorm room, where he died in his sleep from alcohol poisoning. His blood-alcohol level was 0.43 when he died. A Travis County grand jury investigating Mark Seeberger's death said pledges indicated that they considered the "ride" and the handcuffing "part of the fun and excitement of being in a fraternity." A grand jury investigated Seeburger's death but said it couldn't indict anyone because the hazing law was too archaic.

That same year in an effort to stop hazing, the University of Texas persuaded almost every fraternal organization on campus – including the Cowboys – to sign an anti-hazing pledge. It was a good effort and may have worked for a short time, but it didn't seem to stop hazing.

In 1987, the Texas Legislature passed an anti-hazing law establishing fines of up to $10,000 and a maximum two-year jail term for those caught participating in a wide range of hazing events, from paddle swats to calisthenics to sleep deprivation. Fraternities called the law too harsh. Strictly interpreted, they said, it would mean that they would be breaking the law if they simply made their pledges stand in a line or forced them to study.

They broke the law anyway. In 1988 Scott Phillips, a member of the Delts, was chased by two pledges who wanted to throw him into a swimming pool as a part of an alleged hazing ritual. While trying to escape, Phillips fell off a cliff and was killed. A grand jury indicted the fraternity for hazing. In a plea bargain, the fraternity agreed to pay a $5,000 fine.

Travis County attorney Ken Oden, figured hazing would vanish after the well-publicized Seeburger and Phillips deaths. But by the fall of 1990, he found that the vast majority of fraternities were still practicing hazing, and "small groups continued to glorify it." Oden announced that he was investigating 23 cases of hazing and illegal activity that had occurred since September 1989, including one in which pledges were required to perform sex with prostitutes in front of a video camera. Every fraternity president was adamant that they were no longer hazing, though rumors were that the fraternities were still doing it. [7]

In 1995, Jeff Seeberger, the father of pledge Mark Seegburger, in an interview after Gabe died, commented, "There are some fundamental problems in Austin. I think the kids don't have much respect for human dignity and human life, irrespective of their religious convictions." He added, regarding the Cowboys' reaction to Gabe's death, "You've got a lot of fraternities protected and attorneys protecting them because it is a big, big money business." [8]

WHAT OTHER UNIVERSITIES ARE DOING

There are some universities that have taken a strong stand against hazing. At the University of Indiana, as soon as the administration confirms a hazing incident, the organization is kicked off campus permanently.

At University of California, Berkeley, the city has a noise abatement law. If there is a loud party, the police serve a warning. The second complaint is penalized with a city fine of $1000. If there is a third complaint, the fraternity or organization is fined an additional $2,000 and is shut down by the police. It has drastically cut down loud fraternity parties, so much so that Berkeley doesn't have much of a problem with Greek organizations.

Some universities are finding it hard to continue justifying the worth of fraternities on their campuses. Idaho State University, in my hometown, abolished fraternities in the early 1990's, eliminated by the President because he didn't see them as positive influences on the University, probably due to hazing. My younger brother, who was the president of the Sigma Kappa fraternity at ISU in the 70's, remarked that by the year 2000 the football and basketball games started having little or no school spirit like they used to because, he felt, the Greeks were no longer on campus. Since then the Greeks have been slowly coming back on campus. More of the school spirit has returned, but along with it came the problems with the Greeks, specifically hazing and drinking.

Middlebury College, a private, liberal arts school in Vermont with an enrollment of less than 2,000, disposed of Greek organizations after a fraternity defaced a female mannequin on the grounds of its house. The college's board of trustees voted in 1990 to replace fraternities with co-ed "social houses."

Patricia Honacki, the assistant dean of students at Texas Tech University believes that "Hazing can't be stopped by the university alone. The students created it, and they need to abolish it."

Students at Ohio Wesleyan sponsored a four-day workshop over a month's time to help new member educators and chapter members move in the right direction. The four-part series ended with each Greek chapter spending a day working on their pledge program with the assistance of outside resources. Sometimes half the problem with hazing is that there is no written program for officers to follow.

More and more schools are placing responsibility on the students themselves, separating themselves from their involvement with Greeks.

The University of Colorado, for instance, has no legal connection to Greek organizations – and no desire to have one. Instead, it has liaison officers who work closely with fraternities and sororities and a student judicial branch.

"We are charged by the university to work with the students on good self-government," says Amber Tetlow, Greek liaison officer at Colorado. "Often your peers are rougher on you than even the university would be."

Students sign "hazing cards" at Southeast Missouri State University, where in 1994 seven men pled guilty and were convicted of involuntary manslaughter after 25-year-old pledge Michael Davis died of blunt trauma to the head from a beating. In signing the hazing card, students promise they will not allow themselves or anyone else to be hazed. They are told they have an obligation to stop it. By state law, hazing is a misdemeanor or felony, depending on the seriousness of it. The hazing card holds them accountable.

"Constant education is really the key," says Lisa Fedler, assistant director of campus activities/Greek life at Southeast Missouri, "and telling students: this does not need to happen to you. We need the individual students to stick up for themselves." 9

The University of Texas isn't the only school that has problems with hazing. It's a nationwide epidemic, and one that's hard to control.

WHAT UNIVERSITY OF TEXAS IS DOING

The University of Texas' strategy is to educate students about hazing and work closely with the national organizations, cracking down on those that violate the law or UT policy. Each year they suspend Greek organizations at UT or put them on probation to keep them in line.

Dr. Sharon Justice, the dean of students at UT at the time of Gabe's death, believed that suspending an organization for five years – a generation of college students as she recommended in the case of the Texas Cowboys – was an effective way to clean out bad eggs.

University of Texas also believes in self-governance, said Sherri Sanders, UT assistant dean of students in the 1990's. After Gabe's death, UT established an Interfraternity Council Judicial Board, which held the authority to put a fraternity on probation. Being a fraternity on probation would generally cripple their social life in that they wouldn't be able to have parties with any of the sororities.

"It gets their attention," Sanders commented.

The fraternity alumni can be either a great support or a huge detriment. Without supervision, fraternities fall into an attitude of being untouchable in a protective cocoon. Though every fraternity has a local alumni advisor, he is rarely seen at the fraternity house except when the fraternity gets in trouble. Fraternity alums, fondly remembering their college days as some of the best times of their lives, typically will dismiss charges of fraternity wrongdoing as nothing more than "boys will be boys." Often when executives at the national fraternity headquarters try to cut down on hazing in their UT chapters, the alumni will block them on it.

"The alumni will simply stand up to the nationals and say, 'If you interfere, we're going to cut off our endowment,' and that's worth thousands of dollars," said Dan Medlin, the director of UT's Interfraternity Council. Medlin admitted that when he went to fraternities to ask them to set up such things as stricter alcohol regulations at parties, "they would snicker behind my back."

What's more shocking is how the university administration goes out of its way *not* to control Greeks. UT didn't have a Greek advisor until 1989. While other fraternities set up party policies for their fraternities, even requiring frats to register the dates and times of the parties, the UT administration has been wary of acting as a moral chaperon. Greek adviser Sherri Sanders said nothing could be done to control private off-campus organizations like fraternities: "Right now, our ultimate penalty for such a group is to suspend it as a registered student organization, which means they can't appear in the school annual or rent a room on campus or play intramurals for a year. And they just look at us and say, 'So what?'"

One of the problems might be the university's fear of fraternities, or possibly the fear of being sued for their negligence. Dean Justice openly acknowledged that if the university issued more regulations governing fraternity behavior, then the university would be more legally liable when one of those fraternities messes up. [10]

WHAT'S HAPPENING NOW?

The new Dean of Students at University of Texas, Dr. Margarita Arellano (pronounced ar-e-a'-no) stated in an interview recently that there are 1000 organizations on campus that they have to track. One way they are doing that is by requiring the officers of each organization to sign an anti-hazing agreement. They also now have three-day orientation, which includes parents in order to educate the incoming freshmen. Every freshman interested in pledging is required to take a class called Greek 101. UT's enrollment now is 45,000, with incoming freshmen numbering 14,000. The Greek population is 4,000.

When I asked if the Texas Cowboys still hazed, she told me she couldn't reveal that information. She did comment, though, that the Cowboys' Alumni Association is very influential with the group and has helped them tremendously in their reformation.

UNIVERSITY OF TEXAS HAZING DEATHS

The following is a list of young people who have died at the University of Texas due to hazing. University of Texas does not recognize Nick McElroy as a hazing death, though it would be pretty undeniable that his death involved hazing.

1. Pledge Nick McElroy, in a Delta Kappa Epsilon hazing in 1928, died from electrical shock when he had to crawl through box springs charged with electrical current.
2. Mark Seeburger, a UT freshman from Dallas, died from alcohol poisoning after downing 18 ounces of rum while one hand was cuffed to the roof of a van during a Phi Kappa Psi incident in September 1986. He was left in his dormitory room and died in his sleep. His blood alcohol level was 0.43 percent at the time of his death. A Travis County grand jury refused to indict anyone.
3. Member (Gregg) Scott Phillips, 21, a UT junior, perished when he fell from a cliff in Lost Creek, running from two Delta Tau Delta pledges intent on throwing him into a swimming pool in September 1988.
4. Gabe Higgins, a 19-year old Texas Cowboy pledge drowned in the Colorado River after participating in initiation drinking games.
5. On November 11, 1998, Jack L. Ivey Jr., a 23-year-old member of Phi Kappa Sigma, died off campus after drinking heavily (alcohol poisoning). At the time of his death, his blood-alcohol level was 0.40.

~25~

CAN HAZING BE STOPPED?

"You can stop hazing," High School Principal Eddy Bonine commented on an ESPN news clip. "Is it still gonna happen out there, not reported? There's still gonna be the incidence. We can't stop that, but what we can do is let those individuals know that if they commit this act, there's gonna be a consequence."

The athletes from Gerlach High School, located a hundred miles north of Reno, experienced a hazing episode during a road trip. It involved hitting with boards and hangars, a four point pin-down, taping eyes closed, squirting tubes of toothpaste down their throats and other things Mr. Bonine didn't want to mention.

Ten kids were suspended from school, the coach was fired, and the football season was cancelled.

The law has been named "The Threat Law." It means the state of Nevada holds a zero tolerance for hazing. Nevada is one of 43 states with an anti-hazing law and is one of 40 states that regard hazing as a misdemeanor. Most states consider hazing to be a misdemeanor. A few others, like Texas, consider it to be a felony. [1]

WHAT CAN WE DO ABOUT HAZING?

Let's put an end to it!

If you're a parent or grandparent, get involved and encourage the administration at your child's school to recognize that hazing can't be ignored. The sooner a school is prepared for it, the better. If there are no rules or regulations against it, look out, because *it will happen* and you'll find yourself unprepared to deal with it.

Hazing doesn't happen exclusively at the college level. It happens in high schools, junior highs and occasionally grade schools. Get involved, you may save a life. You may save a child from psychological humiliation or emotional damage that could stay with them the rest of their lives.

The goals would be different in universities than in high schools.

At the college level, pledgeship needs to be made a challenging, positive experience. Many fraternities have become alcohol free; some have shortened the pledge semester to a two-week period and some, to one day. Anti-hazing programs need to be taught, along with confronting. Bystanders need to become activists, all schools need to have an anti-hazing policy, and team functions need to be supervised.

In the meantime, fraternities and sororities can make several positive choices that allow for developing camaraderie and unity of the organization. There are many recommendations, which can be found on websites and in books, which are listed at the end of this chapter. [2,3]

One suggestion that I would personally like to recommend, which is something that more universities are implementing is that the Greek system and other organizations be held accountable for their *initiation* practices.

I would go a step further and recommend instigating an additional organization (especially in large universities that are seen as party schools, like UT, who have problems controlling the Greeks) who would be accountable *to* the university, but not *of* the university, specifically hired to investigate and keep tabs on the initiations and wrongful practices of some of the Greeks (and other organizations).

For instance, if an organization is on probation for paddling, like the Texas Cowboys were, I'm recommending that a third party could be hired to keep a check on that organization and report it to the school. Jake Fisher was completely correct in his assessment that if someone was selling drugs or in the business of illegal prostitution, the police would be in on it and it wouldn't be tolerated. So why do we tolerate hazing? Why should it solely depend on a student signing his name to a complaint, a step that might jeopardize his college education or ability to get a job later?

It seems wrong that it should be left up to the students to blow the whistle when someone else could be hired to report on it. It would not only free up the university from that responsibility, it would hopefully cap some of the misconduct, the objective being to stop hazing.

The two arguments against that would be:

1. It might get expensive. Considering that we're talking about life threatening circumstances or possible lawsuits, it wouldn't be. It's called accountability.

2. It might push the hazing activities "underground." What is it doing now? When education hasn't stopped it, go to the next step.

WHAT CAN YOU DO ON A PERSONAL LEVEL?

When hazing happens, ask yourself and make the following inquiries of each activity:

1. Is alcohol involved?
2. Do active members refuse to participate with the pledges and do exactly what they do?
3. Is there a risk of injury?
4. Do I have any reservations describing this activity to a jury, to my parents, to the university, or to the chapter advisor?
5. Does the activity risk mental or physical abuse?
6. Would we object to the activity being photographed by the school newspaper or filmed by the local TV news crew?

If the answer is "yes" to any of the above, then the activity is probably some form of hazing. [4]

Resources include: www.stophazing.org, which not only contains a wealth of information, news, updates, and other links, but includes many books on hazing as well as videotapes, which can be ordered from that website.

I would also recommend any of Hank Nuwer's books:

1. *Broken Pledges, the Deadly Rite of Hazing,* 1990: the story of Chuck Stenzel, the son of Eileen Stevens who started the organization C.H.U.C.K., newly in reprint and available. This book is an encyclopedia of information about hazing.
2. *Wrongs of Passage, Fraternities, Sororities, Hazing, and Binge Drinking:* 1999, also reads like an encyclopedia about hazing, including a wealth of information, history of hazing, and many stories, including Gabe's, with recommendations for reform. Nuwer lists 28 different sources of information (including websites) and

eight pages of books regarding hazing.
3. *High School Hazing*, 2000: an in-depth look at high school hazing and what can be done about it.
4. *The HAZING Reader*, 2004: a collection of enlightening exposes regarding hazing.

Another great resource and organization is called MASH: Mothers Against School Hazing. It was started by Karen Savoy and can be found on the website: www.mashinc.org. This website also includes many other books, videotapes, and DVDs about hazing.

~26~

PERSONAL ADVICE TO PARENTS

WAKE-UP CALL

Get involved! If your child is going to be in any organization, whether it is joining a fraternity or sorority in the Greek system at a university, or being on a high school football team or joining the band in junior high, don't be afraid to check into it. Ask your school administration where they stand on hazing and if they haven't yet taken a stand against it, hand them this book and the addresses of the websites listed in the previous chapter. Ask them to get informed. Ask them to order some books for their staff and teachers and to get a couple of DVDs on hazing. Go a step further and ask them to educate the kids about it. If they won't, maybe you could or should.

Don't let your child join an organization knowing that there is going to be drinking and hazing without getting informed and involved first. Question their policies on initiations and be a burr, or thorn in their sides. Don't let it slide by without looking into it. Educate yourself on the subject, then educate your children on it. Let them know they can say: "NO! I won't do that!" ... before it's too late. Let them know they *should* say: "NO! I won't do that!!"

Your involvement may save their lives, *or* someone else's!

It's interesting to note that there are some who think that hazing is OK, that it develops camaraderie and weeds out the undesirables because they may not show they are strong. My take on it is that those people seem to have endured hazing that hasn't been life threatening or emotionally damaging to them or anyone close to them. Possibly they haven't yet experienced how quickly it can take a turn to the worse and emotionally injure someone for life. In my opinion, anyone who condones hazing embraces a cowardly, bullying and abusive mindset.

Each time Gabe pledged a fraternity, first the Kappa Sigma fraternity, then the Texas Cowboys, I naively thought that since hazing was illegal and archaic, and because there were laws against it, that hazing no longer existed: it had been abolished. I thought that I didn't need to worry about it. After all, (I was sure) the university certainly wouldn't allow such behavior if it was *that* dangerous!

I also trusted in my son's judgment. I hope by reading this book that you now understand how the initiate's judgment and mindset can become warped and victimized into thinking they are safe, when they're not. It wasn't Gabe's lack of judgment that killed him, it was his blind trust.

I learned the hard way that hazing is a real enemy and it's after our kids. It's your duty as a parent to look into it and protect them if you can, even when they've become young adults. Allow Gabe's death to be *your* Wake-up Call.

My deepest prayer is that you won't have to go through what I went through.

EPILOGUE

Blowing In The Wind

When you were just a young boy
Fishing on the dock,
Hooks were unimportant.
Underoos and a cape made you invincible,
And water made you a fish.
    Trees were for climbing,
    And sand was stuff you rolled in....
    Your young locks
    Golden and curly,
        Blowing in the wind.

Later, my love, you stole my heart:
You were teachers' pride and joy,
Shakespeare spoke the lines you loved.
    The hoops you jumped to,
    The sports you excelled in
    Only made me proud you were mine....
        Your young locks
        Dark and curly,
        Blowing in the wind.

Then you left for greater things
That made me even prouder.
Life was hard for you,
    But you met the challenge!
        When you came back, you were a man.
            And, oh, your talent stole my heart!
            You sang now with guitar
                Expressive songs of life and love ...
            Your sweet locks
                Dark and curly,
                Blowing in the wind ...

Lay silent now
NOT to rest
Still ... my best.
Where were the angels then?
No river will look the same to me
No cowboy my delight.
What was taken from this world
One moonless wild night
Haunts me still.

The fruit of my love lies still now
The mystery knows no end.
You never said goodbye, my love.
I'm not sure my heart will mend
From the memories of your golden locks, flowing, curly,
Blowing ...
      Blowing in the wind.

            Ruth Harten
            March 15, 1996

EPILOGUE

Murky Waters

Where were the angels that moonless night?
    The river dark and murky.
      Fighting and swimming after drinking two nights,
    Water moccasin lay lurking.

"Hand over your keys, we'll take care of these,
    Eat this hot dog (with tobaccie),
      Down this beer and race with Mad Dog,
    Trust us now." Forget Mackay.

Cattle prods, branding, selling ads for money,
    Drinking, paddling, hazing, parties,
      "The babes will love you, doors will open for you,
    Drink up, all you college smarties."

They did what they were told to do,
    They wanted so to "belong;"
      But the game soon changed, the flavor darkened,
    So hard now to show they're strong.

One didn't come back, swallowed by the river,
    Their defense: "Boys will be Boys!"
      Does no one know what happened there
    Amid the chaos and the noise?

Rich boys cry "Daddy! Help!
    Come and save your son!
      It was all his fault, not ours!"
    The damage already done.

The daddies chime: "No fear! Keep cheer!
    We've hired the best money can buy
      To hide the truth, we must agree
    In secret, we will lie."

THE COWBOYS' SECRET

And lie they did, it almost worked
    Save one important thing.
  An all-knowing God saw all that night
    Most clearly, that fateful spring.

It only takes one man of integrity
    To set the record straight.
  Yet if there were, this one's for sure,
    They'd stand at prison's gate.

His blood cries out — from peaceful rest?
    That justice was betrayed,
  While cannons blaze, in drinking maize
    Under academic guise.

Dust to dust and ashes to ashes
    Life to death births here.
  The image of John Wayne's stature,
    Fallen, muddied and unclear.

Most cowboys work hard, play hard, too —
    The epitome of time
  That some so deserving of credit
    Should reap rewards of crime.

Memories tainted, lies believed,
    The truth lies dormant still,
  As dead as his decayed body
    Six feet down. The chill.

Oh Most High God, hear my prayer:
    A mother's cry of grief.
  Let no others die such senseless death,
    Behind hidden clouds of sheath.

EPILOGUE

Surely You can take this sour stench
      And remove this ugly stain
   That one sweet life lost tragically
      Would not be in vain.

Tell me God, does truth abase
      When no one stands for honor?
And darkness covers water deep,
      Where then is life?

    Ruth Harten
    1999

FOOTNOTES

I have changed the names of seven people in this book: the five young men most responsible and two young women. When referring to any of those people in these footnotes, I have only used their initials. I also used the initials of those Cowboys who encouraged Gabe to join the Texas Cowboys.

CHAPTER 4 – THE TAPPING IN

1. Interview with Jon Faulkner, Gabe's roommate.
2. There were four Kappa Sigma Texas Cowboys plus two graduated Cowboys, using only their initials: CH, PC, BR, BM, graduates JH & RG.
3. Answers to interrogatories from Steve Casella, Cliff Condrey, and CB, plus Gabe's friend's interviews.
4. CB's Answers to Interrogatories.
5. Statement from Oldman Andrew Thomas.

CHAPTER 5 – PLANNING THE CONCERT AND THE PICNIC

1. CB's Answers to Interrogatories and statement
2. John Welsh's statement (Newman)
3. John Welsh's personal interview with the author, May 1995.
4. Sean Kiehne's statement (Oldman)
5. Todd Shapiro's statement (Newman)
6. Alfred MacDaniel's statement (Oldman)
7. Sean Nimmo's statement (Newman)
8. Jed Buie's statement (Newman)
9. John True's statement (Newman)
10. Jason Hicks' statement (Oldman)
11. Andrew Thomas' statement (Oldman)

CHAPTERS 6, 7, 8 & 9

These Chapters were originally one chapter. Most of the information in this section came anywhere from three to ten different sources. They are listed in chronological order, but all sources were used throughout.

1. Todd Shapiro's Statement (Newman)
2. John True's Statement (Newman)
3. Todd Kinsel's Statement (Newman)
4. Cliff Condrey's Statement (Newman)
5. Brett Hogan's Statement (Newman)
6. Matt Cooper's Statement (Newman)
7. Travis Cagney's Statement (Newman)
8. Sean Kiehne's Statement (Oldman)

FOOTNOTES

9. GG's Statement (Oldman)
10. CB's Statement (Oldman)
11. James Morgan's Interrogatory (landowner)
12. BM's Statement (Oldman)
13. Marc Sachs' Statement (Oldman)
14. Jeff Peterson's Statement (Newman)
15. Robby Belamy's Statement (Newman)
16. Matt Henahan's Statement (Newman)
17. Jed Buie's Statement (Newman)
18. Mike Alfred's Statement (Oldman)
19. Jason Hicks's Statement (Oldman)
20. John Welsh's Statement (Newman)
21. Mark Roberton's Statement (Newman)
22. Guy Ladetsky's Statement (Newman)
23. Alfred McDaniel's Statement (Oldman)
24. Patrick Howard's Statement (Newman)
26. Sean Nimmo's Statement (Newman)
27. Luke Ellis' Statement (Newman)
28. Brian Feld's Statement (Newman)
29. Brad Harris' Statement (Newman)
30. Dylan Lawrence's Police Interview (Newman)
31. Scott Newberry's Statement (Newman)
32. Jason Hick's Statement (Oldman)
33. Todd Shapiro's Police Investigation notes (Newman)
34. Jason Lamin's Statement (Newman)
35. Scott Grossman's Statement (Newman)
36. Steven Cassella's Statement (Oldman)
37. David VanDervan's Statement (Newman)
38. Guy Ladetsky's Statement (Newman)
40. Jimmy Lederer's Statement (Oldman)
41. Marc Sach's Amended Statement (Oldman)
42. Scott Archer's Statement (Newman)
43. Brian Seitz's Statement (Oldman)
44. Lawyer Jeff Rusk's Investigation Notes
45. Author's personal Interview with John Welsh 3 1/2 weeks after Gabe died
46. Jacob DeLeon's Statement (Newman)
47. Mitchell Fagelman's Statement (Oldman)
48. Matt Henahan's Police Interview (Newman)
49. Graham Turney's Statement (Oldman)
50. Texas Rangers' Report
51. Texas River Authority's Flow Chart & Report
52. Matt Cooper's Police Interview (Newman)

53. Patrick Howard's Police Interview (Newman)
54. Todd Kinsel's Police Interview (Newman)
55. Jimmy Lederer's statement (Oldman)
56. John Welsh, personal interview (Newman)
57. Sean Nimmo's addendum to his statement (Newman)
58. Guy Ladetsky's Police Interview (Newman)
59. Notes by Tim Higgins (Gabe's father) regarding a conversation he had with Newman John Welsh, 5/31/95.
60. Phil Kline's statement (Oldmen)
61. Jamie Moore's statement (Oldmen)
62. Ari Purcell's statement (Oldman)
63. Timothy Revell's statement (Oldman)
64. Andrew Thomas' statement (Oldman)
65. Police notes

CHAPTER 14 – WHAT REALLY HAPPENED TO COWBOYS

1. Jim Hawley's telephone interview with my lawyer's investigator on December 27, 1997
2. Presidential Commission on Fraternal Organizations at The University of Texas at Austin, October 9, 1987, pg 80a.
3. Lance Watson's deposition, January 22, 1997
4. Jake Fisher's written document, September 8, 1995
5. Ibid 3.
6. Ibid 3.
7. Scott Scarborough's telephone interview with my lawyer's investigator, December 17, 1995
8. May 3, 1985 – *Daily Texan*
9. Ibid 7.
10. Ibid 1.
11. Ibid: 8.
12. Ibid 4.
13. Ibid 1.

CHAPTER 15 – WHO'S SON WILL BE NEXT

1. Friday, May 5, 1995 – *Austin American-Statesman*; written by Debbie Graves
2. Friday, May 12, 1995 – *Houston Chronicle*; written by Mark Smith.
3. Friday, May 5, 1995 – *Austin American-Statesman*; written by Debbie Graves
4. Thursday, May 4, 1995 – *Daily Texan*; written by Sholnn Freeman
5. Thursday, May 4, 1995 – *Austin American-Statesman*; by Debbie Graves
6. Friday, May 5, 1995 – *Daily Texan*; written by Caleb Canning
7. Saturday, May 13, 1995 – *Austin American-Statesman*; by Debbie Graves
8. Tuesday, June 7, 1995 – *Daily Texan*; written by Michael Brick

CHAPTER 16 – KICKED OFF CAMPUS

1. Tuesday, June 13, 1995 – *Austin American-Statesman*; by Debbie Graves, "UT Uncovers hazing, bans Texas Cowboys."
2. Tuesday, June 13, 1995 – *Daily Texan*; written by Michael Brick, "Texas Cowboys get 5-year suspension."
3. Wednesday, June 14, 1995 – *Daily Texan*; written by Michael Brick, "Hazing probe proceeding slowly."
4. Thursday, June 15, 1995 – *Austin American-Statesman*; by Debbie Graves, "Civil liability is key issue in hazing case."
5. Friday, June 23, 1995 – *Austin American-Statesman*; by Debbie Graves, "Texas Cowboys' appeal stalls UT suspension over hazing."
6. Friday, June 23, 1995 – *Daily Texan*; written by Michael Brick, "Cowboys Move to appeal suspension."
7. Monday, July 24, 1995 – *Daily Texan*; written by Michael Brick, "Cowboys' Appeal reviewed in secret."
8. Tuesday, July 25, 1995 – *Daily Texan*; written by Michael Brick, "Cowboys' Violations upheld."
9. Tuesday, July 25, 1995 – *Austin American-Statesman*; by Starita Smith, "UT ruling on Cowboys' violations upheld."
10. Thursday, July 27, 1995 – *Daily Texan*; written by Michael Brick, "Cowboys' Suspension shortened to 3-years."
11. Thursday, July 27, 1995 – *Austin American-Statesman*; written by Mike Todd, "UT Cowboys' suspension reduced to three years."
12. Thursday, July 27, 1995 – *Austin American-Statesman*; written by Mike Todd, "UT Cowboys' suspension reduced to three years."
13. Friday, July 28th, 1995 – *Daily Texan;* written by Chris Parry, "Rap sheet."
14. Monday, August 7, 1995 – *Daily Texan*; written by Michael Brick, "Justice to appeal decision."
15. Thursday, September 14, 1995 – *Daily Texan*; written by Kevin Fitchard, "Vick reinstates Cowboys' 5-year suspension."
16. Thursday, September 7, 1995 – *Daily Texan*; by artist Chris Panabrer, "Editorials."
17. Friday, September 15, 1995 – *Daily Texan*, picture by Chris Panabrer
18. Monday, September 18, 1995 – *Daily Texan*; "Viewpoint" by Editor Robert Rogers, "Cowboy Cartoon."
19. Thursday, August 31, 1995 – *Austin American-Statesman*; by Debbie Graves, "Parents sue UT group over pledge's death."
20. Friday, September 15, 1995 – *Daily Texan*; written by Kevin Fitchard, "Silver Spurs to fire 'Smokey' at Pitt game."
21. Texas Cowboys Alumni Website at Texascowboysalumni.com
22. Ibid: 20
23. Thursday, February 8, 1996 – *Daily Texan*; written by Renae Merle, "Cowboys

not indicted in drowning."
24. Thursday, February 8, 1996 – *Austin American-Statesman*; by Mary Ann Roser, "No indictment is issued in drowning of Cowboys pledge."
25. Thursday, February 8, 1996 – *Houston Chronicle*; by Mark Smith, "Grand Jury clears UT spirit club in drowning linked to hazing."
26. Monday, February 19, 1996 – *Daily Texan*; written by Renae Merle, "Cowboys want to block release of UT inquiry."
27. Monday, February 19, 1996 – *Daily Texan*; by Robert Rogers, "Open Records."
28. Sunday, March 3, 1996 – *Austin American-Statesman*; by Mary Ann Roser, "Deadly Games: Files shed light on UT pledge's drowning."
29. June 23, 1996 – *Daily Texan*; written by Renae Merle "12 More Texas Cowboys Added to the Civil Lawsuit"
30. June 23, 1996 – *Austin American-Statesman*; by Mary Ann Roser, "Parents Expand lawsuits Against UT Spirit Group"

CHAPTER 17 – LORD OF THE FLIES

1. Golding, William, *Lord of the Flies*, 1954

CHAPTER 20 – HAZING DEFINED

1. http://www.stophazing.org/aboutus.html
2. Nuwer, Hank, *Wrongs of Passage: Fraternities, Sororities, Hazing, and Binge Drinking*, Bloomingdale: Indiana Press, 1999
3. Tuesday, June 7, 1995, *The Daily Texan*; by Michael Brick
4. Franta, Darron E., (Winter 96/97), The Kappa Alpha Journal, *"Cain Slew Abel, Hazing: The Fratricide of brotherhood."* And Ibid: 1.
5. Ibid: 2, and Keim, Will, Ph. D., *"The Power of Caring"* (website: willkeim@proaxis.com)
6. Nuwer, Hank, *Broken Pledges, The Deadly Rite of Hazing*, Longstreet Press, Inc., 1990, pp 236-237, and www.stophazing.org/fraternity_hazing/index.htm
7. Ibid: 2.
8. Tuesday, May 9, 1995, *Austin American-Statesman*; by Ricardo Gandara
9. Ibid: 2.
10. Ibid: 8.
11. Ibid: 4.
12. Ibid: 8

CHAPTER 21 – BULLYING

1. Nuwer, Hank, *High School Hazing, When Rites Become Wrongs*, 2000, pp 56, 57.
2. www.bullypolice.org

CHAPTER 22 – BINGE DRINKING

1. Conversation with Diane Stinner in June 2003; also author was on *Maury Povich Show* with Diane Stinner in fall 1998.
2. March 9, 1997, *Cumberland Sunday Times-News*, Cumberland, Maryland; Sunday; written by Jeff Alderton

CHAPTER 23 – HAZING STORIES

1. May 19, 2003, *Newsweek*; and October 2003, *Oprah Winfrey Show*; Suzannah Meadows & Dirk Johnson.
2. Fall, 1998, *Maury Povich Show*, author was on the show with Jim Knoll and his father, also Jim Knoll.
3. Walker, Robin *You Can Sleep When You Die*, unpublished.
4. Hornbuckle, Bruce, 1988, *Death By Hazing*, Eileen Stevens, SAE, 1988
5. Ibid: 4, and www.stophazing.org: excerpt from Eileen Stevens' speeches.
6. Nuwer, Hank, *Broken Pledges, The Deadly Rite of Hazing*, 1999, pp166-117

CHAPTER 24 – PROBLEMS AT UNIVERSITY OF TEXAS

1. Hollandsworth, Skip, (March 1991), Texas Monthly, *"The Greek Way"*
2. Sunday, June 18, 1995 – *Austin American-Statesman*; Editorial
3. Ibid: 1
4. Ibid: 1.
5. Saturday, March 15, 1997 – *Austin American-Statesman*; by Mary Ann Roser, *"Deadly Games"*
6. Ibid: 1, pg 121.
7. Thursday, May 11, 1995 – *Austin American-Statesman*; by Debbie Graves
8. Thursday, March 20, 1997 – *Austin American-Statesman*; by Bob Banta and Mary Ann Roser.
9. August 30, 1995 – *Austin American-Statesman*; written by Leigh Hopper
10. Ibid: 9.

CHAPTER 25 – CAN HAZING BE STOPPED?

1. *TV News Special*, ESPN, March 2004.
2. Hornbuckle, Bruce D., Sigma Alpha Epsilon, "*Death by Hazing*," 1988.
3. Nuwer, Hank, *High School Hazing, When Rites Become Wrongs*, 2004.
4. Nuwer, Hank, *Wrongs of Passage, Fraternities, Sororities, Hazing and Binge Drinking*, 1999.

ISBN 1412085683

Made in the USA
Lexington, KY
02 August 2013